Over the past few months, Dr. Charles Rolls has appeared dozens of times on the daily international telecast, "100 Huntley Street." He is in his 98th year and his mind is as sharp as it ever was in his prime. His sense of humour, clarity of thought, and total commitment to his Lord and Saviour, Jesus Christ, provide evidence of the unique favour of God upon him. I am convinced that God has spared him and kept him with a mighty hand so that he could minister to this generation as He is doing so powerfully.

This is the third book in the series by Dr. Rolls on the names and titles of Jesus Christ. We take great pleasure in bringing these books to you and pray that God will give you unusual insight as you read them. My pattern is to read one name and its commentary each night. Sometimes I'll read it again the next morning before going to work to let it sink more deeply into my consciousness. This is not light reading, but it is well worth the discipline. The Scripture says, "Whatsoever things are true, whatsoever things are honest, whatsoever things are just, whatsoever things are pure, whatsoever things are lovely, whatsoever things are of good report; if there be any virtue, and if there be any praise, think on these things" (Philipians 4:8). *Time's Noblest Name* is worthy of our full concentration that we might, as the Scripture says, "Grow up into Christ" (Ephesians 4:15).

David Mainse
Host of "100 Huntley Street"

CROSSROADS
CHRISTIAN
COMMUNICATIONS

In Canada:
Crossroads Christian
Communications Inc.,
100 Huntley Street
Toronto, Ontario M4Y 2L1

In the U.S.A.:
Crossroads Christian
Communications Inc.,
Box 4100
Rockford, Illinois 61110

TIME'S NOBLEST NAME

The Names and Titles of
Jesus Christ
L. M. N. O.

by Charles J. Rolls

LOIZEAUX BROTHERS
Neptune, New Jersey

REVISED EDITION, JANUARY 1985

Library of Congress Cataloging in Publication Data

Rolls, Charles J. (Charles Jubilee), 1887—
    Time's noblest name: The names and titles of
Jesus Christ: L—O. Revised edition.

    1. Jesus Christ—Name. I. Title. II. Series:
Rolls, Charles J. (Charles Jubilee), 1887—
Names and titles of Jesus Christ.

BT590.N2R616   1985   232   84-14825
ISBN 0-87213-733-3

PRINTED IN THE UNITED STATES OF AMERICA

To my wife

Mary Kathleen Rolls

*who assisted me in reading through
the first three volumes
to make the necessary corrections
for reprinting*

this volume is dedicated

CONTENTS

N

O

When considering the personal preeminence of Christ the Lord, we can ill afford to disregard His more prominent names and princely titles if we desire to appreciably comprehend in some degree His stately honor. These superior designations throw a flood of light on the suitability of His character for revealing the Father, the sufficiency of His resource for furnishing the requisites of salvation, and the sovereignty of His power for subduing the opposing forces of evil. We are again to devote our attention, and we trust direct our affection, to the contemplating of One whose aims and claims are highest and holiest, and concerning whom all human estimates are immature and inadequate. None can fully know and wholly grasp the mystery of Christ's infinity and the majesty of His glory.

The effulgent dignity of His distinction and the ineffable durability of His dominion eclipse all our standards of calculation. He ranks loftiest in solitary splendor as the Originator of life, the Emancipator from sin, the Liquidator of debt, the Regenerator of men, the Designator of peace, the Vanquisher of death, and will yet be manifest as the Consummator of the age.

From whence do these superhuman qualifications arise? We should remember that the credentials of Christ's capabilities are not conferred by earthly counsels or by national institutions. The bounteous gifts He dispenses so generously are not the product of trust corporations or billionaire benefactors. The potentialities and prerogatives He exercises are not sanctioned by the princedoms and kingdoms of mankind. His complete control of eclipses, equinoxes, and seasons is not a grant made by profound physicists or famed men of science. The legacies of His incorruptible inheritance are not gratuities from commercial banks. The glories of His governmental administration are not subject to any earthly authority. We may affirm confidently that in the widest, weightiest, and worthiest heights of heavenly honor, Christ stands supremely superior in relation to every rank of distinction and noble office. We are well able to speak of Him as the incomparable, indescribable, indispensable Christ.

> His names are glorious in their wondrous claims,
> His titles famous in God's vast domains;
> His light is lustrous to the utmost bound,
> His words most precious in the realms of sound.
>   C. J. ROLLS

INTRODUCTION

The personality of Christ is the most prominent and most significant in the knowledge of mankind. This pertains not only to the whole range of history, but also to the entire region of prophecy and throughout the complete realm of verity.

The Bible as a volume is virtually a portrayal in picture, parable, and purpose of His multiform abilities, manifold activities, and magnificent achievements. In the first five governmental books comprising Genesis through Deuteronomy, Christ is foreshadowed in scores of prefigurements. In the historical section constituting Joshua through Esther, He is foreseen in numerous forms of presentation (for example, Josh. 5:13). In the poetical section containing Job through the Song of Solomon, He is foreknown in various degrees of perception (for instance, Job 19:25). In the prophetical section containing Isaiah through Malachi, He is foretold in descriptive detail proclaiming His many ministries. Wherefore His great and gracious personal character is foreshadowed, foreseen, foreknown, and foretold.

The expectancy that had been awakened by this agelong testimony is adequately answered through the actual manifestation of Christ recorded in the four Gospels. Matthew declares what He said as the King in His dominion. Mark discloses what He did as the Heir in His domain. Luke defines what He felt as the Priest in His devotion. John describes what He is, the Creator in His deity, the One by whom all things are made and maintained. In these four instructive and illuminative messages, He is described by Matthew as wielding the regal scepter, which denotes His supreme authority in Heaven and on earth. He is depicted by Mark as wanting His regalia, which constitutes the rents of properties of the crown which are rightfully His as the Heir (see Lev. 25:23). He is displayed by Luke as wearing the miter, even the High Priest forever, after the order of Melchisedec, an office He holds without predecessor or successor. He is declared by John as witnessing to the insignia which bears the Father's spiritual seal, expressed as on the crimson crest of redeeming love, verifying forever His illimitable power as Creator.

In the Old Testament, the ten leading titles of deity are used over ten thousand times, while in the New Testament, which is a document that may be read through in eighteen hours, the five main names and titles of Christ occur over three thousand times. No other volume in the world is so saturated and pervaded by one chief, central, governing personality as are the Scriptures of truth.

We are aware that there are millions of illustrious names in the galleries of the great, yet His Name is above every name. Are there not also myriads of kingly heroes recorded in the annals of historic kingdoms? Yet He is the King of kings. Is there not a multitude of renowned magnates registered in the famous halls of nations? Yet He is Lord of lords. Are there not legions of divinities revered among the peoples of the earth? But He is the God of gods. Superlative statements such as these are not applicable to any other personality save Christ the Lord.

Because of the interest that has been awakened throughout the English-speaking countries relative to the titles of Christ as dealt with in *The Indescribable Christ* and *The World's Greatest Name*, we now send forth volume three, trusting that this record also of our Saviour's dignified names may be as well received as the former two.

L

Christ is the Summit of all superior splendor and the supreme Sovereign of the centuries. By virtue of His steadfast throne He secures the everlasting satisfaction of His redeemed people.

The LEADER (Isa. 55:4)
> The chiefest in chivalry and constancy.

The LORD OF THE HARVEST (Matt. 9:38)
> The Promoter and Possessor of all that is precious.

The LORD OF LORDS (1 Tim. 6:15)
> One who is almighty in ability and activity.

The LION OF JUDAH (Rev. 5:5)
> Courageously conspicuous in conquest.

The LAST (Isa. 44:6)
> The incalculable and immeasurable One.

The LAMB OF GOD (John 1:29)
> The gentlest and greatest of the gracious.

The LADDER FROM EARTH TO HEAVEN (Gen. 28:12)
> Love's link between the lofty and lowly.

The LOVER (John 13:1)
> The affectionate love of One altogether lovely.

The LILY OF THE VALLEYS (S. of Sol. 2:1)
> The loveliest and lowliest of the lovable.

The LOWLY IN HEART (Matt. 11:29)
> The disposition and deportment of deity disclosed.

The LOFTY ONE (Isa. 57:15)
> Holiest in might and humblest in manner.

The LORD AND SAVIOUR (2 Pet. 1:11)
> Our Lord's distinction and devotion in sacrifice.

WHOSE DOMINION IS AN
EVERLASTING DOMINION

To His omniscience there is no orbit
To His excellence there is no end
To His sovereignty there is no shoreline
To His lordship there is no limitation
To His dominion there is no demarcation
To His compassion there is no circumference
To His blessing there is no border
To His glory there is no grave

THE LOVE OF CHRIST WHICH SURPASSETH KNOWLEDGE

Time may crumble earth's loftiest towers,
   And wither the limbs of the cedar's bowers,
The weather may rust the world's noblest bridge,
   And scatter to dust each mountainous ridge,
But the splendors of love can never die,
   Her beauty and glory outlast the sky.

Heroes may gain a remarkable crown,
   Cities may rise to gigantic renown,
Yet ruin and war consume them as stubble,
   Leaving behind but a graveyard of rubble,
But love's golden chalice abideth for aye,
   Our Lord's name and fame can never decay.

Empires may wane and their glories all fade,
   Nations demise with the laws they have made,
The clashings of steel and strivings of war,
   Pass from the earth to return nevermore.
His love still abides and shines as the light,
   Dispelling all darkness, peril, and night.

Great kingdoms may rise to enslave the earth.
   Famines may stalk with their pitiless dearth,
The heavens may pass with a thunderous crash,
   And lightnings destroy with their blinding flash.

But the love of the Lord immortally true,
  Will ever remain and its pledge renew.

His love cannot fail whatever betide,
  The fullness of God will always reside.
Greater than mountains, oceans, and tides,
  More brilliant than stars and planets besides.
The center of loveliness, beauty, and grace,
  The glory of godhead shines from His face.

C. J. R.

I am Alpha and Omega (Rev. 22:13)

In all the great essential values and eternal verities of high rank and noble office, Christ is preeminent. We may amass the most estimable titles and the most excellent names that are emblazoned in the annals of history but we find that His Name is above every name. Should we contemplate those who are highly distinguished in kingly majesty and regal authority, we arrive at the conclusion that Christ soars loftily above every other principality and power to the utmost degree of superiority, because He is the King of kings and Lord of lords. If we consider the princeliest of governors who have helped consolidate the transient empires of this world, Christ by far outshines their princeliness as the Prince of the kings of the earth, yea, the venerable Prince of Peace, for "of the increase of His government and peace there shall be no end" (Isa. 9:7).

Paul, that Christian philosopher, for so he was, when writing that wonderful message to the church at Colosse, contributes a most worthy tribute to the matchless dignity of Christ (Col. 1:12-23). He states quite clearly that the sublimest fact in the preeminence of Christ consists in His relation to godhead, which He demonstrates in the work of creation. He also shows that the supremest function of His preeminence is revealed in the work of redemption, which He accomplished by the process of crucifixion.

At the summit of a whole set of startling disclosures, when Paul is expressing the spacious and stupendous declarations relative to Christ's creative activities and redemptive abilities, he affirms in one all-inclusive and descriptive sentence the final goal, "that in all things He might have the preeminence." In the light of the context, the monumental meaning of these massive words requires no curtailment or correction, for the verities of Christ defy all statistics, the virtues of Christ defer all estimates, the values of Christ decry all tabulation, and the victories of Christ deter all appraisement.

The manifestation of the Saviour displayed in the four Gospel narratives presents Him in Matthew preeminent in sovereignty as King; in Mark preeminent in sufficiency as Heir; in Luke preeminent in sympathy as Priest; and in John preeminent in superiority as Son. This fourfold portraiture also emphasizes preeminence in the majesty of His prevailing as Conqueror, the mastery of His prowess as Controller, the ministry of His purpose as Conciliator, and in the mystery of His prerogatives as Creator. He is separated by infinite distances in His stateliness of dignity and dominion, far above the status of every other potentate or principality. In preciousness the Son of man surpasses all other estimates of loveliness, in gracefulness He exceeds all other standards of gentleness, in genuineness He excels all other calculations of goodness, and in considerateness He outvies all other valuations of tenderness.

If we turn to the final unveiling in the book of the Revelation of Jesus Christ, the same stately preeminence is everywhere apparent. He first appears in His dependability as Revealer (Rev. 1—3); second, in His distinguishability as Redeemer (Rev. 4—7); third, in His desirability as Reconciler (Rev. 8—13); and last, in His durability as Regenerator (Rev. 14—22). These sections in turn reflect His preeminence in Lordship relative to the Church, in His Heirship in regard to creation, in His Kingship in relation to the commonwealth, and in His Judgeship in respect to the cities. These four vocational honors are reflected in the four camps of Israel. They are also depicted in the four Gospels and portray the four branches of administration under the dominion of a reigning Christ, and He must reign "till He hath put all enemies under His feet" (1 Cor. 15:25).

The four battalions of His army have always been and still remain under one single command. Our Lord's credentials of regal might, legal right, royal merit, and primal light are coexistent, and by virtue of these He is in the exercise of supreme authority in four official capacities at one and the same time, namely administratively as Lord, with His enduring scepter; governmentally as Heir, with His entitled regalia; mediatively as Priest, with His exclusive miter; and adjudicatively as Judge, with His expressive insignia.

Some are prone to take a wrong viewpoint of Christ's preeminence and consider the present hour as a contradiction of such prestige, a view which is sure to cause disappointment and discouragement. They draw attention to the national outlook in the East and dwell on the prevalent state of the Chinese, Japanese, Ceylonese, Javanese, Burmese, Melanese, and Balinese, which peoples comprise about two billion of the world's population, and then ask if this feature savors of Christ's being preeminent in all things. Yes, for in the first place all races receive from Him life and breath and all things, and secondly, this present order is merely a transient phase "for the things seen are temporal," and all things that can be shaken shall be shaken, whereas His glories abide through the ages.

Let us take a deeper, higher, broader look into the reality of the actual facts concerning Him. We may state with full assurance that the Lord Christ is entirely supreme and wholly preeminent in every lofty and lasting sphere of administration. This pertains equally in the celestial, creatorial, astronomical, equinoctial, governmental, spiritual, and judicial realms. Let us engage our attention with a selection of our Lord's titles beginning with the letter L.

THE LEADER

Behold, I have given him for a witness to the peoples, a leader and commander to the peoples (Isa 55:4).

Thanks be unto God, who always leadeth us in triumph in Christ (2 Cor. 2:14).

What a renowned retinue of remarkable leaders engraces the records of national history! Standing out conspicuously at the threshold of every great turn in the trend of momentous national events, we find some distinguished personality. At the Hellespont we meet Xerxes; at the Rubicon, Julius Caesar; at Troy, Hannibal; at Trafalgar, Lord Nelson; at Gettysburg, Lincoln; and at Atlanta, Sherman.

Yet withal, if we scan the whole range of leadership, Christ is not only foremost, but is the most fascinating character of all, chiefest in chivalry, capability, and constancy. The majestic skill and masterful strategy of His wisdom expressed in a manifold variety of ways mark Him out as the most competent and conspicuous of all leaders.

In His capacity as Guide and Guardian He is fully conscious of the challenge of circumstances, perfectly courageous in facing corrupt conditions, and more than chivalrous in confronting the counsels of evil, yea, much more so than any other governing authority. As Lord of leaders He is undaunted by enemy defiance, undismayed by the powers of darkness, undeterred by the scourge of drought, and undisturbed by the ravages of death. Furthermore, the resources of Christ are likewise unlimited, the range of His knowledge is uncircumscribed, the rule of His authority is unconfined, and the resoluteness of His will unobstructible. What an illustrious demonstration of His leadership is given when promoting the national emancipation of Israel from Egyptian servitude.

"[He] made His own people to go forth like sheep, and guided them in the wilderness like a flock. And He led them on safely, so that they feared not" (Ps. 78:52-53). This was no vague and venturesome enterprise such as men undertake, but a perfectly planned project with a definite objective in view absolutely sure of realization. In His leadership He chose the sites of the forty-two encampments, furnished the requisites required, frustrated all enemy designs, framed the social and national laws for their welfare, formed a formidable army for defense, featured His abiding presence and provision in a tabernacle, and forthwith secured to the people a delightful inheritance. During the journeyings the Lord developed the character of His people by discipline, disclosed His beneficent purpose with its divine intent, and demanded their devoted loyalty in all things.

The nation enjoyed in each of the forty-two journeys and encampments the benefits of His Shepherdhood, the beneficence of His Saviourhood, the blessings of His Priesthood, and the bounties of His Kinghood in unstinted measure. This intrepid Leader of Israel is superior to all surroundings for He created all things. He surmounts all obstacles as the Almighty One, He subdues all opposition because of infinite strength, and supplies the need of His people omnipotently as Jehovah-Jireh. He shielded the host by day and safeguarded it by night, He supported the weak and sustained the strong, He sheltered the camps from the burning heat, and secured the congregation from blighting harm. Unlike all other promoters, the position of control He holds and His power of command can never be surpassed or usurped because He is noblest in nature, highest in honor, foremost in fidelity, loftiest in love, wealthiest in wisdom, mightiest in merit, gentlest in grace, and greatest in glory.

No tempest of raging revolt can turn the tide of the prevailing triumph of His leadership. No terrors can thwart the trend of His theocracy in governorship. No turmoil can ever threaten the tenacity of His immutable will in judgeship. No troublous times can terminate the trustworthiness of His throne or deny the truth of His title to Lordship. Christ does far more than lead His people in paths of righteousness and by waters of restfulness (Ps. 23). He leads heavenward, homeward, Godward where the measureless floods of endless pleasure completely satiate the perfected souls of the glorified, in a deathless society. Yea, He leads to a celestial city, a holy habitation, a peaceful paradise, a happier home, a heavenly heritage, a divine domain, even to an eternal estate in a wondrous world beyond. Amid these traceless depths of everlasting delights with their trackless lengths of love eternal, and far beyond the topless heights of holiest aspiration, He ever leads in highways ablaze with light effulgent, aglow with joy abundant and adorned with peace resplendent.

By virtue of His boundless ability, this Leader ratifies a permanent covenant that is immutable, reflects a perfect character that is immaculate, retains a prevalent control that is irrevocable, radiates a potent charm that is irresistible, reveals a poignant claim that is irrefutable, renders a prevenient care which is inimitable and regains a preeminent command which is immortal. What a Perfect! What a Pilot! What a President!

THE LORD OF THE HARVEST

Pray ye, therefore, the Lord of the harvest, that He will send forth labourers into His harvest (Matt. 9:38).
He that sat on the cloud thrust in His sickle on the earth and the earth was reaped (Rev. 14:16).

Boaz, who was the benefactor of Bethlehem and a mighty man of wealth, presents in his princely personality a suggestive portraiture of the Lord of the harvest. But the real harvest over which Christ has supreme supervision is far greater than all the combined grain fields of this universe. He, as the perfect teacher, lifted the figure of harvest to nobler heights and applied it to His worldwide project, which would continue unto the end of the age. We are granted a sight of His stately splendor in the book of Revelation, where He appears with His golden coronet of rightful claim as Reaper of the earth, seated upon a cloud with a sharp sickle in His hand (Rev. 14:14). The cloud as a chariot indicates His absolute independence of human imperialistic authority and of earthly institutions, to either sanction or substantiate His rights and resolutions. As Lord, He is sovereign in power and purpose, privilege, and prestige. Let us recall that in the record of John's message, the Lord's brethren sought to persuade Him to go to Jerusalem for the celebration of the feast of tabernacles which followed the ingathering of harvest and treading of the vintage, but He answered, "Mine hour is not yet come." The words used in this connection, such as vine, harvest, reap, and wrath, direct our attention to final issues (Rev. 14—15).

In the light of Christ's ultimate Lordship of the finality of harvest, let us revert to the familiar setting of His world plan as given by John. "Jesus saith unto them, My meat is to do the will of Him that sent Me, and to finish His work. Say not ye, There are yet four months, and then cometh harvest? Behold, I say unto you, Lift up your eyes, and look on the fields; for they are white already to harvest. . . . One soweth, and another reapeth" (John 4:34-35,37).

Christ saw before Him a stricken world, whelmed in sorrow and stunned with grief. The anguish of man's agony burdened His heart; therefore, in His commission, He envisaged the whole of mankind and enwrapped humanity in His yearning desire, saying to His disciples as He did so, "Go ye into all the world, and preach the gospel to every creature." He may well have vindicated His righteousness by the obliteration of all evil and by sweeping its unholy brood into oblivion. But He delights in mercy and demonstrates His love toward us in that while we were yet sinners, He died for us (Rom. 5:8).

With prescient eye He saw the striking outlook, the sensational opportunity, and the sure and certain outcome. He held the prerogative and power to organize the disorganized, to harmonize the disrupted and to stabilize the disquieted in peace forever. His is the final voice of authority on the foremost need of mankind, for He is Lord of the harvest. When He gave the words of Matthew 9:38 to His disciples and they carried out His instruction by praying, He called the very twelve that prayed. These twelve Jesus sent forth (Matt. 10:1,5). So it was with the four young men who spent a night of prayer for missionary work beside a haystack in a field in Boston. All four were commissioned to go, Adoniram Judson being one of them. This became known as the haystack prayer meeting.

What a glorious array of majesty lay behind our Lord's gracious ministry so unobserved by the leaders of His day. He descended to the lowest that He might ascend to the highest and secure gifts for men which were necessary in fulfilling His appointed task (Eph. 4:8-11). In His descent He submitted to unutterable agony and secured inestimable authority, for He said, "All power is given unto Me in heaven and in earth" (Matt. 28:18).

Wherefore, celestially and terrestrially He is universal Lord and wields the power to govern the wind and waves, to open and to shut doors, to kill and to make alive, to remit or retain sins, to create or destroy, to alienate or reconcile, to judge or justify, yea, power to shrivel the heavens like a scroll. He holds the scepter of supremest authority and sublimest administration and His management is magnificent. His Lordship as Lord of the harvest is most creditable. He gave to the field the faithful sowers and famous reapers, the virtuous testifiers and valiant translators, the studious writers and strenuous workers, the eminent martyrs and excellent missionaries, the hardy heroes and happy heralds, the fervent intercessors and ardent interpreters, together with the silver-tongued and sympathetic-hearted preachers. He fashions many of His servants from the most unlikely material and no other world leader ever adopted so feeble a method and such frail instruments for so mighty a project, for He purposes to subdue all things unto Himself.

With His practical strength and providential skill He is sure to prevail. The grandest work in this world is to be a distributor for the Lord of the harvest, to be under His orders and superintendence, to obey His will, to do His work, and be a participant in that final joy of harvest-home. Remember all power is vested in the hands of the Victor of Calvary, all authority is committed to the Conqueror of death, His injunctions are as insistent and imperative today as ever. Let us not say that the strongholds of superstition are impregnable. We are under a perpetual obligation to this Master to go and teach. Let us calmly consider His commission, carefully investigate its incentive and closely examine the far-reaching extent of His great emprise, "Go ye into all the world . . . to the end of the age." Our vaunted attainments are of no value in His eyes. Spiritual equipment is the great essential. If we believe He has all power as Lord of the harvest, we should certainly obey the proposition He propounds and prosecute the project committed with the utmost diligence and devotion.

Is this the time, O Church of God, to cry, retreat?
And arm with weapons weak and blunt
The men and women who have borne the brunt
Of Truth's fierce strife?
Is this the time to halt, when all around horizons lift,
New destinies confront? Strange duties face our nation;
Never wont to play the laggard when God's will was found.
So rather strengthen stakes and lengthen cords
And to thy kingdom come for such a time.
Great things attempt for Him, great things expect,
Whose love imperial is, whose power, sublime.
                                                    STOKES

THE LORD OF LORDS

Which in His times He shall show, who is the blessed and only Potentate, the King of kings, and Lord of lords (1 Tim. 6:15).

The title Lord, which is rendered from the word *Kurios,* occurs 376 times in the first five books of the New Testament. Over one hundred of these appear in the Acts of the Apostles, eighty of which have direct reference to Christ Himself. Lordship pertains to those who hold the right to administer in some sphere or capacity, whether it be social, national, or spiritual, wherefore Christ's superlative office entitles Him to supreme administrative power over all other authorities. We may picture Him where we will, He predominates everywhere as Lord of legislators, Lord of lawyers, Lord of liberators, Lord of light-bearers, Lord of leaders, Lord of laborers, Lord of lovers, Lord of life, yea, more, He is Lord of lords, and Lord of all (Acts 10:36). The arresting declaration is overwhelming for it assures lordship in every sphere of rule, every realm of power, in every dominion, every empire, every kingdom, every government, and in every administration.

This dignified station of supremacy rests upon self-abnegation. Christ declared to His disciples, "If any would be great among you let him become servant of all." Peter affirmed, "He hath made this same Jesus whom ye crucified both Lord and Christ." So the Anointed One is the supreme Administrator and His authoritative post is brought to light and arises out of an accomplished reconciliation. Christ bears the signet of office and wears the insignia of title to Lordship in far vaster realms than those now visible. Man's unaided mind could never have conceived the range of Christ's administration which is disclosed in the revelations of Scripture, or have calculated the magnitude of resourceful authority reposed in His hands. Thrice in the New Testament the statement is made that He is Lord of lords.

We are familiar with this Lordship in relation to life, light, and love, wherefore the longevity of life, the luminosity of light, and the liberality of love are legislated under His supreme command. Christ made some massive claims during His earthly ministration and declared He had power over all flesh (John 17:2), over all the powers of the enemy (Luke 10:19), and over all that are in the graves (John 5:25). The Apostle Paul in corroboration of this writes, "For whether we live, we live unto the Lord; and whether we die, we die unto the Lord. For to this end Christ both died, and rose, and revived, that He might be Lord both of the dead and living" (Rom. 14:8,9). Christ Himself, the ascended and glorified Lord, confirmed to John on Patmos the reality of His power to raise the dead (Rev. 20:12-13). By virtue of His investiture as Lord of lords, He outlives all other administrators. He outlasts all other authorities and He outvies all other aspirants of world dominion, "world without end," amen.

In order to secure some faint idea of the magnitude of Christ's administrative Lordship, let us scan some of the more familiar aspects unfolded in the Scriptures of truth. Christ is Lord of counselors, creation, and covenants; Lord of abounding providences and abiding privileges; Lord of the vastness of nature and the varieties of nations; Lord of measureless grace and matchless glory; Lord of the beauteous flowers and bounteous fields; Lord of unbounded resurrection power and unblemished righteousness; Lord of delightful comeliness and distinctive compassion; Lord of all racially and Lord of all redemptively (Acts 10:36); Lord of heaven and earth (Matt. 11:25); and also Lord of the harvest (Matt. 9:38).

In His lustrous loveliness of divine likeness, glorious in holiness and gracious in helpfulness, He fulfills the administrations of His limitless Lordship constantly and considerately, and is always mindful of details in dispensing both justice and mercy. Let us revel in this reality that He who bared His own breast to the fiery darts of the devil and bore the brunt of battle against betrayers, who defended His unstained soul with the invincible sword of the Spirit and the invulnerable shield of Truth, is now set down at the right hand of the majesty on high, immortally and immutably the Lord of lords. The qualities of conquest and virtues of victory which attend the Conqueror in His continual exercise of power, verify His teaching and assure His everlasting reign in righteousness.

Already the exquisite brilliance of His blessedness and beauty is infinitely incalculable. The enhancing magnificence of His might and majesty is invincibly inviolate. The excellent effulgence of His radiance and royalty is inconceivably iridescent. The eternal transcendence of His triumph and transfigurement is incontestably immemorial. The exclusive semblance of His preciousness and perfection is become intrinsically immortal, and what shall we say more? The ultimate of His unlimited Lordship is inevitable, for all conflicts must cease, all fetters fall, all persecutors perish, all tyrannies terminate, all evils end, and even death itself must be destroyed. For He will gather together in one all things in Christ, where there is neither Greek nor Jew, circumcision nor uncircumcision, Barbarian, Scythian, bond nor free, but Christ all and in all (Eph. 1:9; Col. 3:11). Whenever we dwell on the capabilities of Christ, the very foresight of His prescience, the vast insight of His providence, and the vital oversight of His preeminence assure the mind forever that He is really and truly Lord of Lords.

THE LION OF JUDAH

Weep not: behold, the Lion of the tribe of Judah, the Root of David, hath prevailed to open the book, and to loose the seven seals thereof (Rev. 5:5).

In the representative figures of lamb and lion in this section of Revelation, we are brought face to face with two of the most formidable facts in relation to Christ. The first of these indicates His sacrificial submission in achieving reconciliation, while the second intimates His supreme sovereignty in able administration. The gracious sympathy of the Sufferer prepares the way for the glorious sufficiency of the sovereign. "Thou wast slain," is a wondrous witness to the costly price paid for the purchase of the power He possesses. In other words, His cross directs to His crown and His crucifixion opens the gateway to His coronation.

In the animal kingdom the fittest figure of meekness is the lamb, while the finest feature of majesty is expressed in the lion. The Creator of the universe, whose work is surveyed and whose will is divulged in the previous chapter, expresses His infinite wisdom in the choice made of these two symbols for the setting forth of the virtues and victories of the Redeemer, and this is done both in regard to His character and conquest. The qualities of His sacrificial grace secure the qualifications of His spiritual government, or we may say His mediatorial mercy as the slain lamb promotes His monarchial majesty as the stately lion. These verities are suitably united in the amazing portrayal before us so as to depict a complete view of Christ in the experience of

His humiliation in sacrifice, combined with the exhibition of His more honorable exaltation to the highest conceivable place of superior sovereignty in the eternal kingdom.

We are permitted a glimpse into one of the most spectacular of the momentous personal acts recorded in any literature, which forms a glowing tribute to the work of the Son of man, who achieved reconciliation absolutely by the sacrifice of Him self. His intrinsic worth and infinite worthiness warrant the weight of worship and the all-inclusive homage which is here rendered to Him as the Prevailer. No other being in the heaven ly realm of holiness and truth had the right to ransom the earth and redeem man. Prior revelation in the Scriptures specified that only the near of kin could fulfill this function in Israel.

Christ entered into this qualifying relationship by becoming man in full identity with the creature and thereby substantiated His right to redeem, whereupon He also undertook to vindicate the law and liquidate the debt on man's behalf. By discharging these obligations, Christ demonstrated Himself as being the only rightful heir who had not forfeited His title of claim to this terrestrial world, and so it is by virtue of this right that He is not only able but worthy to take the title deeds and thrust out the usurper together with his thralldom of death. His credentials in so doing are specifically stated in the description given of Him, "The Lion of the tribe of Judah, the Root of David." Significant symbolism this, specifying the royalty of His nature in heirship, and stipulating the renown of His name in headship.

Primarily Christ created this world, purposefully He re deemed it, presently He will perfect it, permanently He will establish it as a possession for His redeemed people, and by His transforming power He will turn the whole estate into a thorn less, tombless, tearless paradise (Rev. 7:16-17). In the light of such prospects, ten thousand times ten thousand angels, namely, one hundred million, take up the strain with thanksgiving in an anthem of adoring admiration. Myriads of perfected saints join in the resonant rapture of resounding gratitude. The measure less firmament chants its contribution in a rhythmic cantata of

celebration to commemorate so sublime a conquest. Teeming
throngs of testifiers tune their voices to join in the thunderous
acclaim of the great *Tersanctus*. The heavens themselves become
articulate and herald forth their holiest harmonies. Ever-widening, ever-expanding, ever-increasing praise develops to an awe-
inspiring degree throughout the spacious realms, filling and
flooding immensity.

In view of such a victory, the fadeless flowers of paradise are
fairer and more fragrant, the potent perfume of the incense is
more pleasing and precious, and the perennial praise of the
purified is more prolific and perfect, yea, the splendid sympho-
nies of the songs are more sweet and stirring and the harmony
of the hymns more holy and hearty in honoring His glorious
Highness. The throne of His majesty is not supported by stone
slabs and marble masonry, but is upheld in perfect poise by the
living ones who are so ineffably glorious. Psalm 99:1 is rendered,
"Jehovah is throned upon the cherubim." Read also Revelation
4:6 with Ezekiel 1:26. Arrayed in the mantle of majestic might,
Christ is enthroned in boundless beauty amid ceaseless felicity,
being anointed with the oil of joy above His companions, and
is in exercise of powers of endless majesty in a reign of fadeless
glory. What an astounding victory is His!

The insuperable strength of Christ in His Lordship as the Lion
of Judah enables Him to save to the uttermost, subdue all things
to Himself, stabilize His kingdom eternally, and satisfy His redeemed forevermore. No force flourishes that He cannot frustrate; there is no might He cannot master, no strength He
cannot subdue, and no power exists over which He cannot
prevail. The position He holds and the power He wields entitle
Him to coordinate the nations by gathering them together in
one, to consummate an eternal union and to consolidate the
everlasting Kingdom. The movements in the chapter are graphic
and clear-cut. Let us trace ten of these which are associated with
the august display:

A signal arraignment—before the throne.
A legal document—a scroll . . . sealed with seven seals.
A special announcement—who is worthy.
A crucial moment—no one able . . . I wept much.
A tribal aspirant—the Lion of the tribe of Judah.
A regal claimant—the Root of David.
A final statement—a lamb as it had been slain.
A moral endorsement—Thou art worthy.
A royal assessment—reign on the earth.
A loyal compliment—worthy is the Lamb to receive.

THE LAST

Thus saith the LORD, the King of Israel. . . . I am the last, and beside Me there is no God. And who, as I, shall call, and shall declare it, and set it in order for Me, since I appointed the ancient people? And the things that are coming, and shall come (Isa. 44:6-7).

Fear not; I am the first and the last (Rev. 1:17).

Christ in His humanity is the Last Adam in federal Headship of the spiritual race. He is also last in deity, which displays His final Headship supernaturally. "Before Me there was no God formed, neither shall there be after Me. I, even I, am the LORD; and beside Me there is no saviour" (Isa. 43:10-11). The laurels of His Lordships are not leased from another and He remains when all else recedes (Heb. 1:11). He abides when earthly systems are abolished (1 Cor. 3:13). He retains all honors of high office because He has no successor to supersede His everlasting superiority. The finality of Christ is equally as wonderful as His priority, for He is both First and Last and this pertains in all degrees of honor, in all qualities of virtue, in all phases of dignity, in all values of merit, in all realms of royalty, and in all spheres of sovereignty, for verily He outlasts because He is everlasting.

The ceaseless expenditure of spiritual energy and the constant ministry of compassionate mercy cannot diminish the abiding fullness of His personal powers. By virtue of the longevity of His ageless life He outlives all other leaders, in lieu of the loving-kindness of His changeless love He outlasts all other lovers, and in view of ceaseless luminosity from the light of His countenance He outshines all other luminaries, wherefore He is well able to see to the completion of His eternal purpose.

In Him we encounter capacities we cannot calculate and meet with dimensions we fail to define. Our limitations are lamentable when we seek to describe the Christ of God. The faithfulness of His lofty majesty, the preciousness of His lowly meekness, and the graciousness of His lawful mediation, far surpass the spacious splendor of the stars.

In that mighty pageant of grace and glory in Revelation, which is so eloquently expressive of the eternal energy and exquisite excellency of Christ, He thrice asserts, "I am the first and the last," and these declarations as shown in each context stand in relation to His three greatest offices of Priest, Prophet, and King. In these dignified vocations He towers highest and is the finality of each as the Last, preponderantly glorious in majesty, resplendently precious in mercy, and transcendently gracious in ministry. No wonder David said, "Thou art my Lord, I have no good beyond Thee."

By virtue of His priority, being the First, Christ's glory is underived and the inevitable sequence of this, whereon equal emphasis is laid, namely the Last, proves that He is totally independent. All that He commences He completes, for He remains enthroned and retains His reign of righteousness in order to consummate His determined purpose.

The title is exclusively Christ's own and bespeaks the uttermost possible in untarnished beauty and unstinted bounty, in high rank and holy renown, "above all principality, and power, and might, and dominion, and every name that is named, not only in this world, but also in that which is to come" (Eph. 1:21). The designation betokens that His will is paramount and immutable so that He cannot be frustrated; that His wisdom is preeminent and incomprehensible and cannot be disputed; that His word is perfect and infallible and cannot be deflected; that His wealth is potent and inestimable and cannot be depleted; and that His work is permanent and indescribable and cannot be destroyed. We are shown in the record which is given to us of the world to come, that Christ rules in stately grandeur as Sovereign, reigns in solitary splendor as Saviour, and in His sturdy sympathy as Shepherd exceeds all former executors.

No presentation of Christ that is given to us is so heartening as the unveiling of His administrative authority in the book of Revelation. Therein as the Last He is garnished with garments of grace and glory (Rev. 1:13). He is ornate with the odoriferous oblations of overcomers (Rev. 8:4). He is draped in the dignified distinctions of devotion. He is magnified with the majesty of mediatorial mercy. He is laden with the laurels of lasting Lordship (Rev. 19:16); He is vested with vestments of virtue and victory (Rev. 19:13); and He is crested with the conspicuous crowns of His copious conquests (Rev. 19:12). Never has anyone appeared who is more worthy of worshipful praise and adoration, robed as He is in spotless righteousness, the sole Regent of eternal redemption. He it is who met the fatal tragedy of Eden with the vital remedy of Calvary, wherefore the Father hath committed all things into His hands.

The divine decree has been revealed that through Him every phase of the counsels of God finds expression, from Him all that is virtuous receives its valuation, and by Him every righteous activity is sure to find realization. Yea, it is by Him that storms are stilled, strife is settled, sorrows are stanched, sickness subdued, because, as the Last, He is the final solution to all the perplexities and problems that confront mankind, whether they be national, social, racial, or moral. The adequacy and finality of Christ's exhaustless powers which are assured by virtue of His eternal freshness and fullness, minister relief and rest to all hearts burdened with this world's problems.

Whatever may be the process, wherever progress is made, He stands at the end in all the fullness of His undepleted powers, His undiminished strength and undismayed might, Himself the bright and Morning Star, the Sun of Righteousness, the First and the Last.

THE LAMB OF GOD

Behold the Lamb of God, which taketh away the sin of the world (John 1:29).

No title advanced concerning Christ attracts more attention and arrests more interest than the winsome designation, "Lamb of God." The portrayal is full of suggestiveness and indicates at once the sacrificial character He assumed, His submissive conformity to the divine will, the sublime comeliness of His nature as meek and lowly in heart, and the sympathetic compassion of the service He rendered when ministering to mankind.

The beauty of the figure also betokens gentleness of deportment and genuineness of disposition, combined with goodness and graciousness in both character and conduct, all of which features are perfectly suited in their application to the Saviour of the world.

In our contemplation of this charming portrayal of the Lamb we are reminded of another aspect well worthy of notice, for we not only stand face to face with the positive graces already mentioned, but on the negative side there is a total absence of all thought of harshness, hardness, and haughtiness in the picture of Christ that is represented herein.

From the earliest times in human history when Abel brought of the firstlings of his flock for presentation, until the record of the marriage supper of the Lamb, the Scriptures supply an ever-expanding detailed description of the sacrificial characteristics associated with the offering of lambs. All the essential values that are indicated by the terms sufficiencies, sacrifices, supplies, sanctities, sureties, and securities are wholly and adequately furnished from the fullness incorporated in that one suggestive name, the Lamb of God.

The absolute sufficiency of an adequate provision being made for redemption is stipulated in the grand declaration of Abraham on Mount Moriah, "My son, God will provide Himself a lamb for a burnt offering" (Gen. 22:8).

The appointed sacrifice of an arranged passover ceremony, to secure deliverance from the bondage of Egypt and protection from the judgment of God, is expressed in a lamb (Ex. 12:3-4).

The abounding sustenance through an authorized perpetuation of daily offerings to insure the requisites for communion and devotion continually, is made available in figure, by an evening and morning burnt offering of a lamb (Ex. 29:38-45).

The assured sanctity of an ever-availing purification which cleanses from all defilement and pollution is supplied through the presentation of three lambs without blemish (Lev. 14:10-14).

The acknowledged surety for acceptable participation in the feast of firstfruits and for guaranteeing replete maintenance was also set forth in the offering of a male lamb without blemish (Lev. 23:10-13).

The abandonment of submission for the achievement of propitiation, in the satisfying of every claim of divine justice for the securing of justification, is likewise made effectual through a lamb led to the slaughter (Isa. 53:7).

The all-absorbing scene at Jordan crowns with glory the whole of the preceding features, for when the Son of man approached, the whole attention of John the Baptist was riveted upon Him and he exclaimed, "Behold the Lamb of God, which taketh away the sin of the world."

The ever-widening, ever-expanding witness to the necessity and efficacy of a perfect sacrifice spans the entire record of Old Testament history, and covers in its range every form of requirement, which includes that of the personal, racial, national, and universal need. Christ pledged to His disciples that they were to see greater things than these, and when we turn to consider the glorious unveiling in the book of Revelation we are greeted with the most glowing tribute of praise that was ever augmented, the whole volume of which is directed to the glories of the altogether lovely One, in His sacrificial character as the Lamb.

A flash summary of the gorgeous panorama in which the title occurs, twenty-eight times in reference to Christ, is all we have room for here. The all-powerful authority of the omnipotence of godhead dwells in Christ in His sacrificial character as the Lamb. He wields the scepter of age-abiding kingship eternally and infinitely in this same character. The Administrator of the laws of the universe, with advocateship in mediation for nations, peoples, and tongues, is through one designated the Lamb. The Almighty, which is and was and is to come, the appointed Heir of all things with complete right and title is likewise the Lamb. The surety for salvation and sanctification, the acceptance as sons before the heavenly throne is all willed and wrought by the Lamb. The Arraigner of the greatest assemblage ever congregated and the Adjudicator of all men and movements is the Lamb. The Alpha and Omega, the Beginning and the End, the First and the Last is none other than the Lamb.

When victory has been gained in war and the high command of a nation is pinning the decorations won for heroism on the breasts of the heroes, the true soldier prefers to present himself in the scarred battle dress in which he fought in order to receive his honor. The priest of Israel, when presenting a burnt offering, was permitted to take to himself the skin of the sacrifice, as a witness to all of the character of the offering made (Lev. 7:8). So likewise the blessed Saviour is forever displaying to the redeemed hosts above the distinctive and colorful marks of sacrifice by which He secured His right of claim as Saviour and reward of conquest as Sovereign. The great High Priest will bear and wear this lamblike feature forever.

The infinite pleasures of the Father's immortal delight revel complacently in the Son's inherent beauties and rest unabatingly in the full-orbed perfections of His best Beloved, who had power to lay down His life and power to take it again by divine decree (John 10:18). Cherubim and seraphim worship and magnify His radiant virtues in all the unvarying steadfastness of their eternal loyalty. Angels and ministering spirits admire and acclaim His matchless character and adore Him incessantly for having established their status forever in undefiled splendor. The redeemed hosts that are qualified to participate in the perfect pageant of those unmarred celebrations relish the sublimity of the Saviour's glory and honor, for it is through His sacrificial love they live, reign, and rejoice evermore. Again we affirm that the sacrificial character of Christ is the criterion that carries with it every office of distinction, every rank of dominion, every title of deity, and every position of dignified honor in a heavenly domain too divine for words to describe.

THE LADDER FROM EARTH TO HEAVEN

And he dreamed, and behold a ladder set up on the earth, and the top of it reached to heaven: and behold the angels of God ascending and descending on it (Gen. 28:12).

And He saith unto him, Verily, verily, I say unto you, Hereafter ye shall see heaven open, and the angels of God ascending and descending upon the Son of man (John 1:51).

This is the only time the word ladder is used in the Bible and the central thought of the figure is a most expressive portrayal of Christ as the One who spans the great breach that intervenes between man and his Maker. The true significance of the way of ascent in its wealth of meaning is vividly interpreted by the Lord Himself at the close of the first chapter of John's Gospel. Mankind stood in need of reinstatement to favor and fellowship with God, from which position he had been severed through sin and alienated because of wicked works. The divinely promoted vision of the ladder which Jacob saw (Gen. 28:12-14) and the nature of his dream predicted the happy hour when the heavenly authority would establish a means of approach to His presence that would be everywhere available for man's return from distance to nearness. The ladder which reached from earth to Heaven represents a person who is imminent in association, as is the Son of man, and also immortal in administration, as the Son of God, with all power in Heaven and on earth.

The capabilities of Christ are therefore immeasurable and He is certainly able to reinstate man into divine favor, which He does by the processes of redemption, regeneration, and reconciliation, followed by reception into the Father's House. These essential requisites appear in the immediate wake of the application of Jacob's vision which Christ made as referring to Himself, and are found in John 2—14. Again it becomes evident that scenes such as these which appear as minor incidents in Old Testament history have a major inner meaning of far higher significance, for in the light of the Saviour's manifestation and ministry, the hidden meaning is discoverable and discernable. Christ came to open to us the more spacious horizons of the celestial realms and to direct our affection to the higher heights of spiritual conceptions (John 1:51).

We can appreciate in some little measure what it must have meant for Jacob, in his flight as a refugee, to learn of the vital link that existed between earth and Heaven, not on the basis of human merit, for Jacob had none, but on the ground of divine mercy through mediation. What a precious privilege it is to know that there is a way of access to God at all times, and an assured audience in His presence. Noble birth and notable attainment do not obtain this right, but confidence in Christ does, for He is the only way to the Father (John 14:6), and His perfect dignity and purity in holiness are His credentials in conducting us into the presence of deity.

Although Jacob was given a real measure of instructive insight into invisible realities, Christ informed Nathanael that he would be initiated into profounder secrets, "Thou shalt see greater things than these," and He immediately imparted enlightenment and indefinable enlargement by informing Nathanael of the innermost significance of the supernatural that was embedded in Jacob's vision. Our Lord frequently reverted to the scenes and symbols of the Old Testament so as to give us a brighter, clearer, richer view of Himself in His manifold vocations. This is so in the use He made of the Temple, the brazen serpent, Jacob's well, the Bethesda pool, the manna, the pool of Siloam, the Shepherd, and the vine.

On this occasion He frankly displays His own omniscience and discloses His omnipresence. He it was who stood by Jacob in his isolation when life seemed shrouded and shapeless, for nothing escapes His notice.

He beheld Nathanael at a time when he thought himself outside the range of observation while musing under a fig tree. Christ is fully aware of the ancestry, activity, and aspiration of these two characters and of every one else, for He knows what is in the heart of all men (John 2:24).

So the picture is actually the prediction of a Person who has the power and prerogative to conduct us into everlasting habitations.

The infinite love of Christ demonstrates a heart interest in those surrounded by a harassing dilemma, as well as those of honest desire who long for nobler, higher, and greater things.

Countless specific blessings are guaranteed by the Lord's generous pledge to Jacob (Gen. 28:14-15), and numberless spiritual bestowments are assured by His gracious promise to Nathanael. Magnificence and mercy are mingled in the ministry of Messiah the Mediator, who opens this highway of life. From the sphere of mystery as Maker of all things (John 1:3), He emerges in manifestation as the Redeemer who takes away the sin of the world (John 1:29).

In His heavenly domain of eternal harmony wherein His matchless dignity determines all activity, He is the One who ordains seraphim as servitors, cherubim as caretakers, archangels as attendants, and a prodigious army of angels to promote His imperial interests for the reconciliation of all things.

Francis Thompson, when contemplating suicide one night on the Thames embankment in London, was suddenly struck by the reality of Christ's words, "I am the Way," and finding the Saviour available, accepted Him, and afterward wrote:

> In the night my soul my daughter,
>   Sigh, clinging heaven by the hems
> And lo! Christ walking on the water
>   Not of Gennesaret, but the Thames.
> When thou art sad, thou could'st not sadder,
>   Cry! and upon thy so sore loss,
> Shall shine the traffic of Jacob's ladder,
>   Pitched 'twixt heaven and Charing Cross.

THE LOVER

When Jesus knew that His hour was come that He should depart out of this world unto the Father, having loved His own which were in the world, He loved them unto the end [or uttermost] (John 13:1).

Five formidable facts relative to the character of Christ are intimated in the first three verses of this chapter, to inform us of the supernatural nature of this wondrous Lover. His divine prescience is stated, "Jesus knew that His hour was come." His distinctive prerogative is suggested, "depart . . . unto the Father." His disclosed preeminence is stipulated, "given all things into His hands." His declared preexistence is signified, "that He was come from God." His dignified privilege is likewise made specific, "that He went to God."

The durability of His devotion toward His disciples is beyond description, and the extent of the love referred to here is not determined by point of time, as if He loved to the end of His earthly ministry, but to an unabating degree. Our Lord's disposition toward His own is the subject of the prophets, "Yea, I have loved thee with an everlasting love; therefore, with lovingkindness have I drawn thee" (Jer. 31:3). Christ lavished love upon His disciples to the utmost degree of intensity and fervency, and with all the immensity of His inherent infinity behind it.

No revenue is so rich in values, no income is so weighted with wealth, and no returns are so profoundly profitable as those resulting from love. Love is the brightest star in the heavenly constellation of virtue, the richest treasure in the celestial courts of the Heaven of heavens and the choicest gem in the precious casket of the Lord's crown jewels. Such love is personified perfectly in the wholesome character of this Lover, who is so kingly in His kindly affection. The dignified love that always characterized the Lord's life and labor adds intrinsic beauty to His purity, immaculate sanctity to His constancy, and immortal sympathy to His sovereignty.

Yea, in viewing His ways at all times, we observe that love crowns the resoluteness of His will with comeliness, coronates the righteousness of His wisdom with kindness, and completes the repleteness of His work with goodness to the uttermost bound of His many activities. Love perfumes the princeliness of Messiah's Name most winsomely and perfects His preeminent fame right worthily, for "Love never faileth" (1 Cor. 13: 8). We should take particular notice of this declaration because in Christ the fact is fully demonstrated. The variations of rendering given to the verse indicate the fullness it contains:

> Love is proof against all things (Canon Evans).
> Love covereth all things (Revised Version).
> Love always guards her trusts.
> Love is not pleased when others go wrong.
> Love has a gracious tolerance.
> Love knoweth how to be silent (Weymouth).
> Love is always slow to expose.
> Love is reliable in emergencies.
> Love is never missing in trials.
> Love's flower petals never fall.

Sixteen features are also given in the chapter of the aims, attitudes, and activities of love, eight of which are negative and eight of which are positive. The eight things love never does are equally as wonderful as the eight things love always does, and both are beautifully exemplified in the life of the eternal Lover. The love of Christ is abidingly faithful in all covenants, attractively graceful in all conduct, amazingly thoughtful in all circumstances, appropriately helpful under all conditions, and is always cheerful and consoling in the cares and conflicts of life. In one of the opening statements of the Song of Solomon it is written, "Thy love is better than wine." No reference is made in this *Tersanctus* to iniquity, transgression, and sin and no mention is found therein of redemption, reconciliation, revelation, or any of the great doctrines of salvation. On the other hand, the words love, loveth, and beloved occur sixty-five times. Nothing intrudes that jars the eloquence of love or that mars the elegance of her beauty. No tears stain the excellence of her loyalty and no fears restrain the effulgence of her liberality.

As if to enhance the theme of this entrancing song, the superb fragrance of His lustrous love is likened to that of bunches of beauteous blossoms, to gardens of gorgeous graces, to orchards permeated with odoriferous aromas which in turn are conjoined with exhilarating air impregnated with immortal sweetness arising from mountains of myrrh, stacks of spices, and fields of unwithering flowers, creating an exquisite environment similar to the savor of a perfect paradise of perfume. Oh, what manner of love the Father hath bestowed upon us! Dr. Chalmers was in the habit of praying as he approached this sacred song, "My God, spiritualize my affections, give me a more intense love for Christ, who loved me and gave Himself for me." Assuredly we may say with the Apostle John, "We love Him because He first loved us. . . . Perfect love casteth out fear."

> Here conscience ends its strife, and faith delights to prove,
> The secrets of thy Father's love and all His grace discern.

Our glorious Bridegroom is absolutely affable, desirable, and lovable, yea, He is altogether lovely (S. of Sol. 5:16). In this spiritual song the character of Christ's love is exhibited in its deepest nature, the charactristics of love are expressed amid the calm of sanctified leisure. The companionship of love is enjoyed as a most valued treasure. The courtesies of love are exchanged in a congenial atmosphere. The constancy of love is exemplified with dignified pleasure. The confidences of love are exercised in restful composure, while the considerateness of love is evidenced in such lavish measure that every capacity is captivated, and perfectly satiated. Christ as a lover is loftier than the highest in stateliness, greater than the worthiest in comeliness, and richer than the wealthiest in gracefulness. What an object for sanctified affection!

"Christ also loved the church, and gave Himself for it" (Eph.

5:25). "Christ also hath loved us, and hath given Himself for us" (Eph 5:2). Three things are impressed upon the mind as we contemplate the verities of these two verses, namely, the perfect comeliness of Christ, the precious companionship of the Church, and the priceless communion of Christians. What an unspeakable favor is bestowed that we should be betrothed to so potent a Lover and so preeminent a Lord (Hos. 2:19-20). "God so loved . . . that He gave His only begotten . . . ."

This assurance bespeaks intimate association with one whose infinite affection cherishes His beloved bride in the loving bonds of immortal constancy. The love of Christ prepares an abiding home, bestows abnormal honor, bequeaths an adorning holiness, and bedecks the soul with His own adorable beauty in a new creation of heavenly bliss. He beautifies His bride and perfects her without blemish, to manifest His own entrancing comeliness, which will provoke and promote the wonder and admiration of angelic hosts (Ezek. 16:14; Eph. 3:10).

The love of Christ is too desirable in the loyalty of its devotion to be even declared, too delectable in the royalty of its affection to be described, and too durable in the reality of its perfection to be defined. What is revealed is written for us that we might know the love of Christ which "surpasseth knowledge," which means nothing less than to know that the one solitary Lover who is altogether pure, abidingly precious, and absolutely perfect, loves us. This is a legacy loftier and lovelier than our limited minds can grasp.

The transcendent measure and transparent motive of Christ's love is the most satisfying that has ever been disclosed to mankind. No parallel can be found throughout the entire range of human history. If we are ever to obtain a comparison to His love we must needs go outside the realms of this world altogether, for divine love has nothing to equal it in this terrestrial scene. The only love that is comparable in caliber and changeless constancy in the entire universe is that of the Father's love to the Son. Christ uses a startling correlative when He states, "*As* the Father hath loved Me, *so* have I loved you" (John 15:9). His crowning prayer is even more wonderful, "I in them, and Thou in Me, that they may be made perfect in one; and that the world may know that Thou hast sent Me, and hast loved them, as Thou hast loved Me" (John 17:23). The shoreless ocean and fathomless depth of this boundless love were replete in fullness and complete in faithfulness before the foundation of the world (John 17:24). In statements such as these the intensity of love is conjoined with immensity, its intimacy is combined with infinity, and its integrity is coupled with immutability.

The entire volume of divine love in its glorious resource and richness springs from the heart of the Eternal One; no outside factor contributes one iota to its priceless values and peerless virtues. The Lord loves because the character, nature, and essence of His being are love. The fragrance of love exudes in the sweetness of His savor, is diffused in the perfume of His presence, reflects in the radiance of His righteousness, shines in the charm of His countenance, beams forth in the bounty of His beneficence, glows in the glory of His goodness, and sparkles in the splendor of His superiority. "Hereby perceive we love, because He laid down His life for us." In each of the considerate and compassionate offices of His Manhood, Saviourhood, Shepherdhood, and Priesthood, we see the enduring excellence of His personal love perfectly and permanently displayed.

THE LILY OF THE VALLEYS

I am the rose of Sharon, and the lily of the valleys (S. of Sol. 2:1).

What a striking picture this is in its illustrative values of a sweet-scented silently sensitive, serenely submissive life. Also suggested in the beautiful figure as related to our beloved Friend, we see reflected some of the graceful qualities that characterize His life and labors. The lily nature would signify the loveliness of His presence, the likeness of His purity, the long-suffering of His patience, and the loving-kindness of His pity richly impregnated with the perfume of His precious Name.

The protrayal of the lily-like character of Christ is an extremely exquisite one. How wonderfully suited the title is to our precious Lover, by virtue of the charming sweetness, comely sensitiveness, and cheerful submissiveness that so characterized His every act and attitude. His vigorous body was vibrant with purity, His virtuous soul was fragrant with beauty, and His victorious spirit was radiant with glory, throughout the entire period of His ministry of mercy and service of sympathy. When the sinless Saviour drew the attention of the disciples to the lilies of the field, He was directing their interest to what has been rightly called "The queen of flowers." An ancient Arabic record affirms that on one occasion when teaching His followers, the Master said to them, "Consider *this* lily and what it is will-lessly be thou willingly." Maybe He uttered these words, but we know most assuredly that He did say, "I came not to do Mine own will, but the will of Him that sent Me," which certainly exemplifies the former statement as being the method of His life, and again, "I delight to do Thy will."

When contemplating the choice range and variety of blooms that confront us in the lily family, with their rich values and rare virtues, we turn our thoughts more especially to the Aram lily with its graceful design, to the silky-white purity of the eucharist or Easter lily, the charmingly smooth enamel-like surface of the water lily, which is known is South India by the name *Vanaruha,* which means, "born in the waters," or the silky luster of the delicate iris in shades of crimson, purple, and white, together with numerous other kinds which lift their specific variety to a high place in the flower world.

In the light of such qualities, what are we to say of Him whose excellence exceeds all other beauty? The perfections of Christ as the Lily of the Valleys are peerless, for He is sublimely superior in His winsome worthiness, and handsomely holy in His fragrant sweetness, which is thrice called in Scripture, "the beauty of holiness." How fair and fascinating are the floral features of His purity, and how lustrous in loyalty is the fidelity of His limitless love.

The comeliness of His changeless constancy and the integrity of His faithful friendship display the real disposition of His divine devotedness, which constitutes one of the many perfect pleasures that attend His abiding presence. In His radiant deity Christ surpasses the form of flowers, for He is in the form of God (Phil. 2:6). In His glorious likeness He exceeds the loveliness of lilies, for He is altogether lovely (Song of Sol. 5:16). In precious fragrance He exceeds the perfume of all blossoms, for His Name is as odoriferous ointment poured forth (Song of Sol. 1:3)! Yea, all other blooms blush in the presence of His unblemished beauty and untarnished purity.

In addition to the attractive delights and charming colors that characterize blossoms, we should not be unmindful of the rich resources that are resident in the flower world. The manufacturer and the merchant, the botanist and the chemist recognize the wealth that may be obtained by devoting attention to the cultivation of flowers. We need but call to mind the many tinctures which are used in therapy, and are obtained from this source; also, the many tons of honey secured therefrom by the bees, the manifold treasures of costly perfume distilled from flower petals, the myriad tracings for designing lace curtains, carpets, drapes, and wallpaper, the memorable teachings on holy humility and godly contentment taken from their nature by the Master of rabbis and the many time and season indicators that announce the hour of the day and month of the year.

So we are not surprised to find that the Creator of such a cosmos of color and comeliness should choose to select symbols from this field to reflect His own sacred character. "I am the rose of Sharon, and the lily of the valleys," is an admirable figure to use for expressing the divine nature, and it takes on a wealth of new meaning when we consider the simplicities of the Son of Mary, the sympathies of the Son of man, the sufficiencies of the Son of the Most High, and the sublimities of the Son of God in one person. We should be altogether spellbound by the charming dignity of His disposition. How greatly our conceptions of loveliness are magnified when we link the unsearchable riches of Christ with the dew-drenched freshness and fragrance of a wonderful rose garden at the dawn of a delightful day.

Is there any occasion in gladness or grief when flowers are inappropriate and unacceptable? They certainly enrich the sunshine of the marriage festival and cheerfully engrace the sorrowful atmosphere of mourning at the funeral ceremony. So likewise there is no circumstance of delight or distress we may ever be called upon to encounter in the which we can afford to disregard His presence or discard His proffered help. What a change His presence can make in the hour of crisis, in the heat of conflict, in the heart of contentment and in the hall of communion.

"I am the lily of the valleys" is like a cordial to refresh the disheartened servant, is a comfort to rejoice the dying saint, and is as a charter to reassure the daring soldier of the Cross. Do we not long to dwell more in the company of a Companion so dignified, and nestle nearer to so notable a Lover, and revel in the society of so distinguished a Friend, in order that we may behold the beauty of the Lord and experience more of the warmth of His affectionate heart of infinite love?

How matchless are the transporting memories of His many mercies! How manifold are the transcendent messages of His mighty ministries! How multiform are the transparent motives of His manly mediation!

THE LOWLY IN HEART

I am meek and lowly in heart (Matt. 11:29).

All too frequently meekness and lowliness are features of character which some think of as being undignified and undesirable characteristics, but meekness is not weakness and lowliness is not littleness. In fact, meekness is never weakness, but the majesty of might harnessed by a Mediator, to be used in ministering the manifold mercies of God to mankind. This combination is indicated at the triumphal entry, "Tell ye the daughter of Zion, Behold, thy King cometh unto thee, meek, and sitting upon an ass" (Matt. 21:5).

Likewise on the other hand, lowliness is not littleness, but the loftiness of supreme Lordship condescending to stoop in loving-kindness to the human level, to live and labor for the uplifting of man that he might become heir to life's largest legacy.

Christ's lowliness is yet another of the loveliest features of His perfect character, to which He Himself calls special attention, and which is identified in the context with some of the most magnificent claims of glory and greatness that He ever made during the manifestation. He had just previously declared, "All things are delivered unto Me of My Father, and no man knoweth the Son, but the Father" (Matt. 11:27). This is followed by a startling claim that is threefold, "I say unto you, That in this place is one greater than the temple . . . behold a greater than Jonah is here . . . behold, a greater than Solomon is here" (Matt. 12:6,41-42). So the One who is lowly in heart is the Manifester of the Father (Matt. 11:27), the Mediator for access (Matt. 12:6), the Messenger of the Word (Matt. 12:39), and the Monarch of kingly authority (Matt. 12:42).

Although glimpses of His unrivaled royalty and regal rights flashed forth at times, like rays of light from a priceless jewel, yet the radiance of His majesty and the renown of His ministry were rarely seen and went largely unobserved, save by those to whom He said, "Blessed are your eyes, for they see" (Matt. 13:16). His high honor and stately sovereignty were wholly concealed from the casual and curious. He did not gird on His sharp sword and ride forth gloriously as King of kings for His time to do so had not yet come. The sacred splendors of His spiritual virtues had been veiled in the body of His flesh. The vital values connected with His most venerable titles were hidden for the most part from natural vision. His period of earthly service was unattended by armies of strength, unaccompanied by courtiers of state, and unsurrounded by servitors of style; nevertheless the laurels of His lowly life and His labors of love live and last forevermore. The Saviour's lowliness was not brought about by any lack of lordship or leadership; His celestial credentials were perfectly clear from His birth.

Most surely Christ demonstrated invincible might in quelling storms, in quenching thirst, in quickening lives, and in qualifying souls for entry into His everlasting kingdom.

He displayed impregnable peace amid the scribes in court, the scorn of the crowds, the scourge of cords, and the shame of the Cross.

He declared infallible truth in proclaiming the Father, in predicting the future, in preaching forgiveness, and in promising His followers eternal recompense.

He disclosed inestimable grace in receiving sinners, in remitting sin, in revealing salvation, and in renewing the strength of His servants.

Verily, in all this activity He displays that He is lowly in heart and lovely in humility, and although in Heaven He is rightly honored by holy hierarchies with the highest tributes of homage, yet in His divine descent to the earth He made Himself of no reputation, and took on Himself the form of a servant. When we consider the nobility of His Name, the notoriety of His fame, and the notability of His claim, we marvel that He should deign to serve and suffer and be stricken for the guilt of man, be wounded for transgressions, and be bruised for iniquities. Why should one so dignified in sovereign majesty wash the feet of disciples or feel the heat of the day? Why should He stoop to borrow a boat, stop to ask for a colt, wear the yoke of service, or bear the stroke of justice and be smitten of God and afflicted? Why should the meekest of mankind, the humblest of humanity, and lowliest of leaders be subjected to wear a crown of thorns and bear a brutal cross and thereon be crucified? One answer only can be given, the Lord of Heaven was lowly in heart, wherefore He endured the cross and despised the shame.

Never before had princely sovereignty and perfect simplicity blended so completely and harmoniously in one person. His lowly attractive deportment, His lovely affectionate demeanor, and His lordly authoritative disposition were equally in accord and in complete agreement. In the case of Christ, lowliness is the actual spiritual character of His person, not something He assumes or acquires. The reality of this disposition is foretold by the prophets. In His submission to sacrifice He was led as a lamb to the slaughter (Isa. 53:7), and opened not his mouth in protest. Zechariah, in describing His manner of approach to Jerusalem says, "the King cometh unto thee ... lowly, and riding upon an ass" (Zech. 9:9).

In a quiet dignity and calm serenity He entered the city as the veritable personification of holy simplicity, and this was so naturally expressed, the boys and girls were attracted and brought a tribute of praise and formed His bodyguard. Imposters and pretenders would never dare adopt the lowly guise of riding on a colt the foal of an ass, but would naturally seek the pomp and pageantry of outward display to make up for their inward moral deficiencies. The decorations that distinguished Christ from all other claimants consisted of moral graces and spiritual glories. He displayed the choicest crown of compassion, He swayed the sincerest scepter of sympathy, He wore the loveliest miter of mercy, while His graceful garments of sacrificial service attracted those who sought for pardon and peace and purity. His method in dealing with His own people is not to alarm but assure, not to confound but console, not to drive but draw, and not to compel but constrain.

Our blessed Lord left the loftiest state of honor and holiness to come into this world and befriend the frail and faltering sons of men and to find that which was lost. If we need any additional proof to confirm the claim He made of being lowly in heart, we find full verification in the gentleness of One so great, in the peaceableness of One so powerful, in the sweetness of One so strong, in the mercifulness of One so mighty, in the sincereness of One so stately, in the faithfulness of One so fair, and in the tenderness of One so true.

THE LOFTY ONE

For thus saith the high and lofty One that inhabiteth eternity, whose name is Holy. . . . I dwell in the high and holy place, with him also that is of a contrite and humble spirit, to revive the spirit of the humble, and to revive the heart of the contrite ones (Isa. 57:15).

This lofty One is the lowly One, for although He is holiest in might, yet is He the humblest in manner, and although strongest in majesty, yet is He sweetest in mercy. The resources of His kingliness are expressed in the riches of His kindliness and His glorious throne is demonstrated in His gracious truth.

The character of Christ which is disclosed in this quotation is one of the chief concerns of divine revelation and considerable space is given to the subject in every section of the Scriptures. We meet betimes with the fidelity of His faithfulness, the constancy of His considerateness, the transparency of His truthfulness, the bounty of His blessedness, the majesty of His meekness, the humility of His holiness, and the glory of His graciousness, which are the incomparable excellencies of His mind and heart that comprise the very nature of His Name, the subsistence of His soul, and the constituents of His character. We have mentioned but seven of the multiform features of His comely personality lest the manifold beauty of a full list of His intrinsic glories overwhelm our capacity. How clearly the Scriptures define His sincerity of heart (Matt. 11:29), His state of mind (Phil. 2:5), His strength of will (John 6:38), His sacred work (John 9:4), His stately wisdom (1 Cor. 1:24), and His steadfast Word (John 12:48). The four constituents with which the incense was compounded contribute yet another portrayal of our Lord's lovely character.

In lieu of the length and breadth and depth and height of such characteristics, even the title Lofty One seems too inadequate in its degree of descriptiveness to designate the utterly superior distinctions of His divine attributes.

Endeavor, if you will, to envisage the dignity of His disposition, the dimensions of His dominion, the durability of His distinction, and learn how impossible it is to describe His honor which rises highest, His Name which ranks noblest, and His Saviourhood which remains the stateliest of any vocation conceivable. Little wonder that the praise of His exceeding excellence as the altogether lovely One is voiced in the Song of Solomon, nor should we be startled with surprise that His superb throne titles are couched in lustrous superlatives such as King of kings, Lord of lords, and God of gods. Furthermore, by what more suitable terminology could the holy habitation of His dwelling place be described, than in that which it is given, namely the Heaven of heavens? The speech used of such realities vainly attempts to express the undefinable altitudes of His unqualified ascendency, which implies that He is beyond the highest heights that are within radius of human knowledge, and that, too, in both moral and spiritual glories, the figure used in Hebrews is singularly appropriate in that it signifies the ineffable, intangible, and inconceivable superiority of Christ, "Far above all heavens, filling all things."

Intensification of utterance and magnifying of resemblance fail to fully depict to our finite capacities the infinities of Christ's deity, which remain incomprehensible in their unbounded, unlimited splendor. Although elegantly enthroned in the exclusive excellence of high eminence in this uppermost station of perfect preciousness, with the uttermost of supremacy His own in all the brilliance of beauty, the beneficence of bounty, and the blessedness of benignity, He is, nevertheless, most mindful of man, for He guarantees the society of His companionship and the company of His fellowship to all who are contrite in heart, humble in mind and lowly in spirit. This is a further demonstration of the sovereignty of His unutterable grace and the sensibility of His unfathomable love, which surpass knowledge.

In essence, this assurance of the indwelling of the Lofty One who inhabits eternity is the golden secret of mystery, majesty, and mercy to which the Apostle Paul refers when he says, "Christ in you, the hope of glory" (Col. 1:27). The Lord of hosts, the Most High , who dwells in the high and holy place, lifts His people to dwell with Himself in the age-abiding association of the highest. This is a secret which prophets and kings could not discover and which even angels desired to peer into (1 Pet. 1:12).

Of the things stated, this is the sum, for the deity of the Lofty

One, the Son of God, to merge with the lowly One, the Son of man, in order to manifest God to man, to mediate on man's behalf, to mitigate human sorrow, and to mercifully meet the soul's deepest need, is the greatest masterpiece of mercy known. Isaiah, in an earlier chapter, which tells of the safety, security, and society of the Lord's redeemed people, writes as follows, "The LORD is exalted; for He dwelleth on high" (Isa. 33:5). Then, following an account of the Assyrian reign of terror, he immediately passes to a note of exultant triumph: "Now will I rise, saith the LORD, now will I be exalted, now will I lift up Myself" (Isa. 33:10).

To this is added, "He shall dwell on high. . . . Thine eyes shall see the king in His beauty: they shall behold the land of far distances" (Isa. 33:16-17). Therefore our heavenly calling means no less than to be called to celestial heights of spiritual maturity, to be perfected in the harmony of unity, the purity of sanctity, the beauty of glory, and the felicity of immortality, with Him.

> Eternal light; Eternal light! how pure the soul must be
> When placed within Thy searching sight,
> It shrinks not, but with calm delight,
> Can live and look on Thee.

THE LORD AND SAVIOUR

For so an entrance shall be ministered unto you abundantly into the everlasting kingdom of our Lord and Saviour, Jesus Christ (2 Pet. 1:11).

God hath made that same Jesus, whom ye have crucified, both Lord and Christ (Acts 2:36).

The Apostle Peter affirmed at the close of his memorable discourse on the day of Pentecost that Jesus was made Lord and Christ. A definite distinction is indicated between Jesus being Lord and Jesus as the Christ. In His rank as Lord He presides in abiding administration over all (Acts 10:36).

He is also the Lord of glory (1 Cor. 2:8) and the Lord of

Heaven and earth (Acts 17:24). His anointing as the Christ signifies that He is possessed and acknowledged by the Heaven of heavens, hence the expression the Lord's Christ (Luke 2:26), and the Christ of God (Luke 9:20; Rev. 11:15). The Saviourhood of Christ is related to His character as Lord, and was so announced by the angels, "unto you is born this day in the city of David a Saviour, which is Christ the Lord" (Luke 2:11). The Apostle John affirms, "the Father sent the Son to be the Saviour of the world" (1 John 4:14). The Apostle Paul stipulates that the acknowledgement of this Lordship leads to the assurance of salvation, 'If thou shalt confess with thy mouth Jesus as Lord" (Rom. 10:9, RV). Peter likewise impresses upon us the need of sanctifying in our hearts Christ as Lord (1 Pet. 3:14-15 RV). Had he not himself endeavored on two occasions, when replying to instructions received, to say, "Not so, Lord"? But such an attitude is untenable, for if we are loyal subjects, we cannot refuse to do what our Lord bids.

Far too many people today pacify their conscience with the idea that they possess imputed righteousness, when all the while they are living lives of indifference to the sanctifying work of the Spirit. Such persons definitely refuse to put on the garment of obedience in all things, in order to secure the white linen raiment which is spoken of as the righteousness of the saints. By this attitude they expose their own self-will and lack of submission to the Lord. Like the guest in the parable, they accept the invitation to the marriage feast but decline the wedding garment. If we desire to partake of the riches of His grace, we must submit to the rules of His grace.

Christ has been exalted with the right hand of God to be a Prince and Saviour (Acts 5:31), wherefore by the full expression of the divine might and the grand exhibition of stately majesty, the Lord Jesus is exalted to the highest and holiest office. Celestial spectators witnessed this celebrated conqueror being coronated, amid surroundings of superb splendor. Moreover, the Apostle Peter informs us that angels, principalities, and authorities were made subject to Him (1 Pet. 3:22). The sight is glorious to contemplate, for the Man of sorrows becomes the Master of seraphs, and the meek and lowly in heart ascends to be Monarch of all lords in Heaven.

In the midst of principalities and powers, He is declared the blessed and only Potentate. Although flanked by a replete retinue of royal attendants, He is the sole Prince of kings. Fitly arrayed in the gorgeous garments of state that no moth can mar, and enthroned before this august assemblage of authorities of noblest caliber, He surmounts all in administration, as Lord of lords.

Mankind stood desperately in need of just such a competent Lord, One who could stem the ravages of death and vanquish ghastly grief of its diabolical powers. Where in the whole wide world is there a luxurious garden without a grave, or a spacious shore without a sepulcher, or a prosperous town without a tomb, or a lustrous city without a cemetery? Why must all natural beauty become blemished, why should physical comeliness be turned to corruption, or why should the precious child and princely courtier alike perish? While scattering about hideous disorder, this ruthless monster shows no pity to the poor, no mercy to the millionaire, and utterly disregards the wail of the widow or the warrior's mortal wound. Where may we turn to find a Deliverer? "Blessed be Jehovah who hath not left us this day without a kinsman" (Ruth 4:14). Yea, and One more kindly disposed than Boaz, kinglier than Solomon, and stronger than Satan.

This is He who of God is made unto us wisdom and righteousness, sanctification and redemption; that, according as it is written, "He that glorieth, let him glory in the Lord" (1 Cor. 1:31). We have good cause to speak magnificently of our Lord, for His Lordship means more than mind can grasp or tongue can utter. We can never exaggerate His glory or exceed His worth in any terms of expression we may use.

> O Lord! there is no peerless Name like Thine,
> Emblazoned on the arches of the years;

Wherein the streams of power and might combine,
To banish death, with all its fears and tears.

M

*No name abides the ages in its sweetness, freshness, and greatness, with
an ever-increasing splendor and an ever-expanding grandeur, other
than the wonderful Name of our precious and glorious Lord Jesus Christ.*

The MAKER (Ps. 95:5-7)
  Capable in His control and constant to console.
The MAN OF SORROWS (Isa. 53:3)
  Smitten of God; stricken with grief, yet He endured.
The MERCIFUL HIGH PRIEST (Heb 2:17)
  His sufficiency and sympathy suffice for all.
The MERCY SEAT (Rom. 3:24-25)
  His majesty and meekness are blended in mercy.
The MIGHTY GOD (Isa. 9:6)
  Superior in His supreme strength and stability.
The MESSIAH THE PRINCE (Dan. 9:26)
  The Prince of princes and Prince of kings.
The MEDIATOR (1 Tim. 2:5-6)
  The Assurer of access and acceptance with God.
The MESSENGER OF THE COVENANT (Mal. 3:1)
  His credentials confirm His commission.
The MASTER (John 11:28)
  Supreme in title, right, claim, and might.
The MINISTER OF THE SANCTUARY (Heb. 8:1-2)
  Generous in the bestowment of every good gift.
The MAINTAINER (Ps. 16: 5-6)
  The Safeguarder and Securer of spiritual substance.
The MAN CHRIST JESUS (1 Tim. 2:5)
  Unique in His understanding and undertaking.

WHAT IS HIS NAME?

In transcendence Christ surmounts all other celebrities
In resplendence Christ supersedes all other royalties
In magnificence Christ excels all other majesties
In effulgence Christ eclipses all other worthies
In valiance Christ exceeds all other deliverers
In excellence Christ outvies all other dignitaries
In endurance Christ outshines all other potentates

WHAT IS HIS SON'S NAME, IF THOU CANST TELL?

The Names of Christ are greater
    Than the measure of man's mind,
His light and love are broader
    And cannot be defined.

The claims of Christ are vaster
    Than space or ocean main,
His titles form His charter,
    Assure His lasting reign.

The fame of Christ is wider
    Than all of royal renown,
He sways the grandest scepter
    And wears the costliest crown.

The plan of Christ is brighter
    Than any man can frame,
His purposes are older
    Yet He abides the same.

The might of Christ is stronger
    Than man will ever know,
He holds all power in Heaven
    And here on earth below.

The right of Christ surpasses
    The rights of all combined,

The Lord, the King of rulers
He cannot be defined.

One radiant hope shines clearest
The Morning Star the sign,
The King will come in glory
And reign in peace divine.

C. J. R.

I am Alpha and Omega (Rev. 22:13)

Neither a philosophy nor a morality, but a history of the Saviour constitutes the good news for mankind, universally. The transient things of this terrestrial world may to some temporary extent gratify the nature, but can never eternally satisfy the spiritual capacities of the human soul. The considerate Creator knew this perfectly well and catered for the complete satisfaction of the creature by sending His Son, who is Heir of all things, and Head of all principality and power, to be the object of our hearts' affection, the overseer of our wills' submission and the overcomer for our minds' adoration. Man had been endowed with a capacity to appreciate constant love, to approve competent power, and to appraise complete wisdom.

By virtue of His lustrous name, lovely nature, and lasting nobility, the Lord Jesus Christ furnishes us with all the fullness of God so that we may be made complete in Him.

If we are to be brought to a full realization of the absolute sufficiency of the Lord, it becomes necessary at times to encounter an experience somewhat similar to that which the disciples met when on the Mount of Transfiguration. Two outstanding leaders who represented ancient systems which had been divinely instituted for human well-being appeared there in manifestation with Jesus. This was in order to remind the disciples of the beneficial part that Moses and Elijah had played in the administration under the old economy. After Christ's followers had witnessed this dramatic display, which was spectacular to a degree and sensational in the extreme, the supernatural vision vanished completely and they saw no man save Jesus only.

Although it may prove an exhilarating tonic to behold the magnificent and gaze upon the transcendent for a few moments, we need a durable foundation for our faith, a reliable refuge for our trust and a notable companion for our confidence. There-fore the solid rock basis of everlasting strength and security is revealed in a living Person, of whom it is written,

> Warm, true, tender even yet, a present help is He,
> And faith has still its Olivet, and love its Galilee.

The systems represented in Moses and Elias and the mount must needs recede, because the old symbolical, typical, and pictorial orders were passing to give due place and preeminence to the new unveiling in the Person of the Son of man. The Law and the Prophets had provided no delivering grace, no saving power, no constraining love, no satisfying possession, no endur-ing peace, no abounding joy, no abiding rest, and no everlasting life, but every one of these realities was now to be centered, as the truth is, in Jesus (Eph. 4:21).

When bereavement invades the family home, and brightness fades from the sky, when kindly benefactors seem far removed, and buoyant health departs, when the voices of the sentimental and the sensational cease to make any appeal, what does it matter so long as we recognize that such experiences as these must needs form part of the divine process which prepares us to look up and see Jesus only. If we seek real cheer or true comfort, or if we desire a faithful guide and a powerful guardian, let us repair to Him alone. All that is most worthy to be revered, respected, and relied upon is resident in the Saviour of the world, and even though all else fades He abides. Although the mountains depart and the hills be removed, "Thou, O Lord, remainest for ever" (Lam. 5:19).

> All things change around us day by day,
> Dear familiar voices pass away,
> Gentle lives that used to touch our own

Pass beyond us to the vale unknown;
And the changing pathway of the years,
Leads us often through a vale of tears.
Only *One* of all, our hearts love best
Stands unchanged, beside us bears the test
Of our deepest helplessness and need.
Bends, to lend a helping hand and lead,
From our loss and loneliness and pain,
To the wealth of His eternal gain.
Only *One* is true and as we turn
From all of earth, 'tis then we learn,
How those things that once did seem,
All our highest good are but a dream,
And even though our cherished idols fall
How, in finding Him, we find our All.

THE MAKER

The LORD is a great God, and a great King above all gods. . . .
The sea is His, and He made it: and His hands formed the dry
land. O come, let us worship and bow down: let us kneel before
the LORD our maker. For He is our God; and we are the people
of His pasture, and the sheep of His hand (Ps. 95:3,5-7).

The brief psalm from whence we have taken our title, Maker,
deals with the claim and control of our Lord's creatorship,
combined with His constant care for His creatures as the chief
Shepherd of the sheep.

The sea is His and He made it, and it still bears the marks of
His might and majesty. The palpitating surge of its alternating
advance and retreat, the perpetual tides rising and falling, its
ever-changing sameness with undulation and fluctuation, heav-
ing and receding are continual witnesses to marvelous workmanship. When He was on earth Christ clearly demonstrated
His Creatorship, for when the gale had lashed the Sea of Galilee
into a turmoil, and its boisterous billows and tempestuous break-
ers hurled their force and foam in all directions, He rebuked the
wind, commanded peace to the troubled waters, and there was
a great calm.

The combination used here of linking together the words *sea* and *sheep* is most fascinating, for both need the Maker's almighty hand to bring them to rest, which is the last word of the psalm we are considering. Also, the two references to "hand" recall the profound statement Christ made when assuring security for His sheep in which He referred to "My hand" and "My Father's hand," concluding His utterance with the claim, "I and My Father are one" (John 10:27-30). Likewise we find linked in this Gospel the sea and the sheep, to which twenty-eight references occur, and withal Christ holds the same relationship as Maker, "All things were made by Him: and without Him was not anything made that was made" (John 1:3).

This matter of Christ as Maker comprises one of the highlights of John's presentation. The message confirms that He made the luminaries of the heavens and the lands of this earth. He made the lamb for Abraham's offering and the ladder for Jacob's reconciliation to God. He made what was lacking at the wedding feast. He made the living well of satisfaction for the woman of Samaria and made the lame to walk at Bethesda's pool. He made the loaves for the multitude by Galilee and liberty for those in bondage to sin. He made the light for guiding the blind, the laver for cleansing the defiled, and the law of loving one another. Likewise, through to the end of John's Gospel the Spirit of God maintains the dramatic portrayal in clear graphic detail, that Christ is Maker of all things and the Maker of man.

He commanded the sea that it should not pass His decree and set the confines of its limited domain, but He did far more for His creatures who had been ensnared into bondage by the devil and sin. For their sakes He determined a strong deliverance based on His own substitutionary death, which was to be followed by a divinely declared entrance into the kingdom of His everlasting dominion. Well might we as the people of His choice, worship and bow down before the Lord our Maker. He loved us and gave Himself for us, therefore the luster of that love will never dim, the glory of such grace will never fade, and the fame of His precious name will never die. He is worthy of the utter-most tribute of thanksgiving and adoring gratitude. The marvel-ous dominion of His divine majesty and the matchless designs of His divine mercy are alike incomparable. When King David mused on the greatness of God's handiwork, he admired the infinite intelligence of the love which created and cherished him and exclaimed, "I will praise Thee; for I am fearfully and won-derfully made" (Ps. 139:14). He who made the myriad stars, the mighty oceans, the march of seasons, and the magnificent land-scapes, has made us fit to be partakers "of the inheritance of the saints in light" (Col. 1:12).

He who is the Maker of every glow of light, every flow of tide, every show of grace, and every row of pearls, made us sons and daughters of the living God.

Yea, and He who mantles the forest with trees, furnishes the fields with grain, floods the air with fragrance, fills the garden with flowers, and flings the flaming sunsets across the skies, has made us kings and priests unto God and His Father (Rev. 1:6). This is His greatest work. What a Maker!

> He fashions every perfect form,
> He guides the stars and rushing storm,
> He molds the precious tiny things
> And gives the eagle massive wings.
> He made the orbit for the sun,
> And all the space wherein to run,
> He formed the sands of every shore
> And gave the rocks their golden lore.
> He draped the landscape with its flowers,
> The shady brook with leafy bowers,
> He wrought the tint of every jewel,
> He made the coal to use for fuel.
> He makes the wounded spirit whole,
> He binds the heart and cheers the soul
> His ways are infinitely kind,
> He soothes the thoughts and calms the mind.
> He made the myriad stars to shine,

He set the ocean's boundary line
For all who on His word rely,
He wields the power to justify.
The Maker of new life, the King,
Who did in truth salvation bring
Who rose in triumph o'er the grave
And reigns on High to guide and save.

C. J. R.

THE MAN OF SORROWS

He is despised and rejected of men; a man of sorrows, and
acquainted with grief: and we hid as it were our faces from Him;
He was despised, and we esteemed Him not (Isa. 53:3).
My soul is exceeding sorrowful, even unto death (Matt. 26:38).

Among the many memorable titles of the Saviour of mankind
none is more arresting and affecting than this one, "A Man of
Sorrows." By virtue of His royal resplendence as Son of the
Highest we could readily understand if He were called a man
of sovereignty, a man of superiority, a man of supremacy, a man
of stability, a man of sufficiency, sensibility, or even of sanctity,
but a man of sorrows seems utterly unsuited to the beloved Son
sent by the Father of glory. The fact remains perfectly true, as
Augustine said, although God had one Son without sin, He has
never had a Son without sorrow, and in this tragic feature Christ
is the preeminent One. If we are observant, we realize that
suffering and sorrow minister to the human race from birth to
burial.

Half a century ago professor Godet said when contemplating
human grief, "If I were God, the sorrows of this world would
break my heart." When Sir Robertson Nicol, who at the time
was editor of *The British Weekly,* heard this, he replied, "So they
did." What insight is permitted us into the nature of divine grief
when we examine Psalm 69. "Because for Thy sake I have borne
reproach. . . . For the zeal of Thine house hath eaten me up; and
the reproaches of them that reproached Thee are fallen upon

me. When I wept, and chastened my soul with fasting, that was to my reproach. . . . Reproach hath broken my heart" (Ps. 69:7,9,10,20).

The Lord exchanged the highest seat of heavenly honor for the lowest state of earthy humiliation and identified Himself with human sorrow in order to remove its very cause. He became acquainted with grief in its severest form, encountered pain in its sharpest pangs, experienced agony in its worst nature and endured desertion of the most cruel kind. Because He was perfect in every capacity of His manhood, He was far more sensitive to sorrow and felt it more keenly than others, and He was more sensible of grief and understood its nature as no one else did.

Can it possibly be that this faultless, guileless, sinless Son of man is a Man of Sorrows? Yea, verily, during the whole period of His earthly manifestation a multitude of grievous burdens lay heavily upon His soul. His was the sorrow of a disowned affinity, He came to His own and His own received Him not; the sorrow of a despised affection, with tear-filled eyes He said, "How oft would I have gathered you . . . but ye would not"; the sorrow of a disregarded appeal, "ye will not come to Me, that ye might have life" (John 5:40); the sorrow of dishonored claims, "ye do dishonour Me" (John 8:49). How poignant was the sorrow of rejected love—so eager, so fervent, more tender and solicitious, yea, more strong and passionate than a mother's love for her child. How painful the sorrow when His own people resented the light of the knowledge of the glory of God that shone forth from His countenance. How personal the sorrow that pierced His heart when the rulers ridiculed His labors as being of the devil. How positive the sorrow which grieved Him when His proffered freedom from the bondage of sin was refused, an fer which was regarded by the Jews as altogether uncalled for, yea, and unnecessary (John 8:32-34).

The gracious ministry of Christ so full of help and healing was hampered by an unreasonable unbelief, hindered by unwillingness to obey, and obstructed by an untoward obstinacy.

Together with these many aspects was the grievous sorrow of being misrepresented in His deeds, misinterpreted in His demands, and misunderstood in His devotion. In every feature He was maligned and mistrusted. Yea, it seemed as though malignity mounted highest and envy enlarged itself in the betrayal of the Son of man. We are appalled at the brazen treachery of Judas in playing the traitor and delivering Him up for silver, the cynical hypocrisy of the chief priests in wrongfully accusing Him as worthy of death; the bitter enmity of the rulers in falsely condemning Him for blasphemy; the sinister jealousy of the Pharisees in rudely denouncing Him as a deceiver; the awful animosity of the Herodians in maliciously misrepresenting Him as an imposter; the rough brutality of the Romans in criminally crucifying Him while He was a victim of injustice.

This heap of insults directs our thoughts to the plaintive cry of Jeremiah, "Is it nothing to you, all ye that pass by? behold, and see if there be any sorrow like unto my sorrow, which is done unto me" (Lam. 1:12). No one before or since has ever been called upon to encounter such heart-rending, soul-saddening, mind-staggering experiences.

When we consider His holy character with its honesty of disposition, nobility of deportment, sincerity of desire, and maturity of discernment, we wonder what He must have felt! The Son of man was called upon to endure the direst onslaught of devilish hatred, the darkest night of deceitful wickedness, and the deepest depths of deliberately designed cruelty ever expressed. Such encounters clearly disclosed that He was the Messiah of prophecy, whose coming had been predicted centuries before and who was to bear the name, "a man of sorrows and acquainted with grief." His cup was more bitter and His path more thorny than that of any other messenger. The awful stigma of becoming a surety for sin, the shameful dishonor of being made a substitute for sinners, the severe scourging with its lacerating stripes for man's healing were all perpetrated by base men, in an environment of withering scorn, with an atmosphere of rancid mockery. The blackest shades of agony crossing over

His spotless soul, His slighted love, His stifled pity, and His scorned benefits, weighed as an intolerable burden upon His heart.

When the celebration of the Passover drew near, a memorial feast which He himself had instituted, He was wholly ignored, and not a single household in Jerusalem had invited Him to participate in the ceremony. This was one of the most unreasonable of the unkindnesses He encountered. Think for a moment of His credentials, the most royal of rulers disowned, the most loyal of leaders despised, the most sincere of sovereigns dishonored, and the most dignified of deliverers was Himself deserted. How deeply genuine was His grief, how profoundly real His sorrow when the tokens of His kindness, the testimony of His knowledge of God, and the trophies of His kingliness were all repudiated and scorned.

The nation in general was sore displeased because of the downfall of the people's own carnal expectations. They believed that Messiah would establish a material kingdom characterized by greater splendor than had previously existed under a Jewish scepter. The rulers of the day were also deeply mortified because the supreme demand Christ made was for a life of moral integrity and practical righteousness, the standards of which they sternly resented. Wherefore, they looked round about for weapons to avenge their disgust, wholly begotten through a misapprehension of the Scriptures, and stumbled into the grievous error of permitting one text to obscure a score of others. Pride was injured and prejudice prevailed, and the nation's rulers definitely believed they were acting in conjunction with the solemn charge committed to their care in Deuteronomy 13:1-2, for they affirmed with great mental emphasis, "by our law He ought to die" (John 19:7). So deeply incensed was the High Priest of Israel that he used the actual balances of the sanctuary to weigh the silver for a settlement of the sordid bargain that had been made with a notorious betrayer. Dishonesty and deceit never showed themselves in an uglier light than under these tragic circumstances. How true are the lines:

Shame tears my soul; my body, many a wound;
Sharp nails pierce these; but sharper that confound
Reproaches that are free, while I am bound,
Was ever grief like mine.

THE MERCIFUL HIGH PRIEST

Wherefore in all things it behoved Him to be made like unto
His brethren, that He might be a merciful and faithful high priest
in things pertaining to God, to make reconciliation for the sins
of the people (Heb. 2:17).

Mercy is what man needs most of all in his relationship with
the Most High. The Hebrew word for mercy is derived from a
root which means to bow, to bend, to stoop, and indicates the
compassionate attitude which the Creator ever holds toward the
creature. In its various forms it is used upward of two hundred
times in the Old Testament, twenty-seven of which are associated with the mercy seat which was above the ark of the covenant. The ark contained God's holy law, so the mercy seat above
it signified that mercy intervened between Heaven's holy law
and humanity's heinous sin.

What heartening news this is from the Most High, which tells
of a gracious Mediator with abundant mercy in His outstretched
hands for mortal man, to safeguard him from the just penalty
of sin. The Lord in His highly exalted dignity, would certainly
need to stoop low even when condescending to speak with a
renowned prince in a gorgeous palace, but a much lower stoop
is necessary to bestow mercy on those abjectly poor and surrounded by dismal poverty.

When the eternal bows the skies
    To visit earthly things,
With scorn divine He turns His eyes
    From towers of haughty kings.
He bids His awful chariot roll
    Far downward from the skies,

To visit every humble soul
With pleasure in His eyes.

Moved by divine love to mediate for man, the Son of God first made the necessary propitiation to meet every requirement of the righteous justice of God. This He accomplished by His substitutionary death on man's behalf and afterward rose again for his justification, ascended for his acceptance and presented Himself in the heavenly sanctuary in all the perfection of His matchless beauty and moral glory as an intercessor to assure ceaseless maintenance. The rendering of this propitiation that Christ both made and paid did not promote or precede the love of God, for the divine love purposed and planned it. Therefore Christ, the anointed One, who has all the imperial might and infinite majesty of Heaven to support His mediative priesthood, is able to minister the tender mercy of God's gracious kindness and compassionate care for the lasting blessing of mankind. Better news than this was never sounded in human ears, for it it the most wholesome and winsome message that was ever vouchsafed to humanity. The angelic hosts on high were amazed at the announcement and praised His Royal Highness for expressing the exceeding riches of His kindness in such lavish measure and in so costly a manner on such as were devoid of merit (Eph. 2:7). Christ expressed these facts to the rulers when He said, "I came not to call the righteous but sinners to repentance."

This merciful High Priest who wears the exquisite miter of effulgent glory despiseth none, He raiseth up the poor from the ash heap and lifteth the needy out of the refuse dump that He may set him with the princes of His people. Oh, what wondrous love and mercy He hath showered on the children of men. We should meditate far more upon His tender mercy and gaze more intently on His kindly grace and peer more earnestly into His wondrous pity until the heart burns with gratitude and learns to sing the melody of that mercy to the music of the spheres. He might have chosen the choicest of cultured minds, the keenest of trained intellects, and the cleverest of refined sensibilities for companionship, but He does not despise dullness nor decry the decrepit. He holds no contempt for inferiors nor does He ignore the hungry and poverty-stricken. He bore patiently with Peter the denier and did not banish Thomas the doubter. He is more glorified in His covenant of grace than He is in His great creation, yea, He is more magnified in the ministry of mercy than in the mystery of His majesty. To think of God as a tyrant is to think of sin as a trifle but to know Him to be loving is to know sin to be loathsome.

The Lord appears to find real pleasure in selecting the despised and ostracized and to bestow on such the rights of heavenly glory. Of old He chose unhewn stones to build a sacred altar and selected the common material of a desert thornbush to express a blazing sunburst of His own ineffable light. He delights to lift the lowest to the highest rank and transform the vilest into the most virtuous. He frequently used discarded and unwanted fabrics to unveil the beauties of His mercy and delicateness of His loving sympathy, just because He is a merciful and faithful High Priest.

His salvation makes the repulsive attractive, by His power the wretched are made winsome, the degenerate are made desirable, the corrupt are made comely, the vicious are made virtuous, and the abominable are made amiable to share the holy association of the saints in light and love eternal. Union with this mitered High Priest who is so majestic in mercy is a richer jewel than the rarest gem ever displayed in a royal diadem. Communion with the crystal-pure Christ outmatches in value the costliest crown and chiefest coronet ever designed. No other privilege in time or eternity could ever equal it.

Have you and I today stood silent as with Christ
Apart from joy or fray of life to see by faith His face?
And grow by grief companionship more true,
More nerved to lead, to dare to do, for Him at any cost?
Have we today thus stood to lay our hand in His and thus compare
His will with ours, and wear the impress of His wish?

Be sure such contact will endure throughout the day,
And help detect within the hidden life sin's dross, it's stain,
Revive a thought of love for Him again,
Steady the steps that waver and help us see,
The footsteps meant for you and me.

Let us remember that our faithful high priest officiates in His mediation and ministration after the order of Melchisedec. A great contrast exists between the Aaronic priesthood of Israel and the Melchisedec priesthood of Immanuel. The status of the Aaronic priesthood was not royal, the range of the mediation exercised was not universal, the character of the sacrifices offered was not spiritual, the merit of the atonement made was not effectual, the function of the office was not perpetual, the ministry discharged was not perpetual, the garments used were not immortal, the sphere of the service was not celestial, the judgment administered was not final, and the glory expressed was not eternal. These comprise some of the striking differences between the two orders.

When we turn to the Son of man, the status He holds is royal (Heb. 7:2,13), the mediation He wields is universal (1 Tim. 2:5). The sacrifice He offered is spiritual (Heb. 9:13-14), the reconciliation He made is effectual (Heb. 10:14), the office He fills is perpetual (Heb. 7:16), the ministry He exercises is perpetual (Heb. 7:17), the garments He wears are immortal (Rev. 1:13). The sphere of His service is celestial (Heb. 8:1-2), the verdict of His judgment is final (John 5:28; Rev. 20:12), while the effulgence of His glory is eternal. Forasmuch as He ever lives and ever loves as a merciful and faithful High Priest, His mercy is everlasting (Ps. 103:17), His consolation is everlasting (2 Thess. 2:16). The redemption He secured is eternal (Heb. 9:12), and the inheritance He obtained is age-abiding (Heb. 9:15). We therefore perceive that all the treasure believers inherit, together with title, right, claim, and merit are fully expressed and finally established by our merciful and faithful High Priest.

THE MERCY SEAT

Being justified freely by His grace through the redemption that is in Christ Jesus: Whom God hath set forth to be a [mercy seat] through faith in His blood, to declare His righteousness for the remission of sins (Rom. 3:24-25).

The word *hilasterion,* rendered propitiation, is the propitiatory or mercy seat, and is so translated in Hebrews 9:5. Twenty-seven references are made to the mercy seat of the sanctuary in the Old Testament, and the figure supplies a significant feature of Christ's priestly character as the Remitter of sins through redemption, and in His becoming the point of meeting God for our initiation into friendship and fellowship immortal. If Christ be the Door into the sheepfold He is most certainly the Mercy Seat of the sanctuary, the One who initiates us into the household of God. The divine will and the divine wisdom conjoin in determining that He should be set forth in this capacity for the full assurance of our confidence and communion. The command was given to Moses, "thou shalt make a mercy seat of pure gold," and the instruction which followed, added, "there will I meet with thee, and I will commune with thee from above the mercy seat" (Ex. 25:17,22).

Then do not let us disregard so dignified a decree, but repair to Christ whom God hath set forth as a Mercy Seat. Through long centuries of history the priests and prophets of the old economy of Israel had prepared the way for this particularly significant revelation of Christ as the Mercy Seat for our sins (1 John 2:2). Moses clearly portrayed the basis on which God planned to banish human sin, bring into being His salvation, and furnish beneficent blessing for those forgiven and justified. Also, the memorable message of Abraham to his son on Mount Moriah mingled the merciful provision of God with the grave solemnity of that sacred hour when he said, "My son, God will provide Himself a lamb, for a burnt offering." This does not say, "God Himself will provide a lamb," but God will provide Himself. After centuries were spanned, the Word that was God became flesh and tabernacled among us, and Heaven's final herald as the forerunner, proclaimed, "Behold the Lamb of God, which taketh away the sin of the world." The Lamb is God Himself, manifest in His sacrificial character for the remission of sins. David expressed this profound reality when He said, "God will redeem my soul" (Ps. 49:15). Not with silver or gold, but He Himself purged our sins, for He bore in His own body our sins on the tree.

This is mercy's deep unfathomed sea, love eternal, love to me. May we be quite sure of this, yea, verily, the star was appointed, the signs were arrayed, the songs were sung by angels, the seals were affixed, the signature was autographed to mark His identity and to assure our hearts that this is He, who, when led as a lamb to the slaughter, offered Himself as a suitable, all-sufficient sacrifice for sin. God now invites me to meet Him and I need have no fear in responding, for the Friend of sinners stands as the point of contact. He has covered my defenseless soul with the shadow of His sacrificial love; my sin was transferred to my substitute, He suffered the just for the unjust that I might be made suitable for divine society and be satisfied in the security of a complete salvation.

What is this? Nothing less than the merit of the blood of Christ, which founds and furnishes the reality of meeting God, forasmuch as God hath set Him forth to be the sole ground of grace, the only medium of mercy, the one platform of peace and the lone basis of blessing for all time. The blood of Christ avails adequately, meeting all claims of divine justice by answering for all my guilt. "He will not justice twice demand, first, at my bleeding surety's hand, and then again at mine." God became man that He might be just and the justifier of the ungodly. Why is this? Because judgment for sin has already fallen upon Jesus which is called Christ and He is set forth as the Mercy Seat. In the wisdom of God it is His option as the Almighty One to offer mercy, yea, He delights in it (Mic. 7:18).

"He delighteth in mercy" was the quotation given by Dr. Alexander Whyte of Edinburgh in response to the inquiry of Dr.

Carmen, the most brilliant lawyer of the city. The statement proved to be Dr. Carmen's introduction to the God of salvation. In the great psalm of thanksgiving the enduring mercy of God is mentioned twenty-six times (Ps. 136). David declares that the disposition of the divine mercy is tender, its degree plenteous, its dimension as high as Heaven, and its duration everlasting (Ps. 103:4,8,11,17). We should cherish the fact that Christ, in His choice and charming character, is the Center, Citadel, and Channel of everlasting mercy.

Who is this? The Prince of princes, the King of kings, the Lord of lords. We beheld His glory, the glory of the only-begotten Son, full of grace and truth. The glory of His people Israel is a statement that takes us down through the aisle of the ages to include the glory of the patriarchs Abraham, Isaac, and Jacob, the glory of the prophets Elijah, Elisha, and Ezekiel, the glory of the priests Aaron and his sons, the glory of the princes Jonathan, David, and Daniel, the glory of the promises of righteousness, peace, and joy everlasting, the glory of the praises in worship, adoration, and thanksgiving and the glory of the purposes, to gather together all things in one. We had all sinned and come short of the glory of God, and Christ came to manifest that glory which had been forfeited. He expressed and demonstrated it throughout His ministry, but as Ruler of Israel He was rejected; as the Key of David, defamed; as the Prince of life, killed; as the Lord of glory, debased; and as the Fullness of the Godhead, emptied and laid in the lowest pit; because He was made sin for us, He who knew no sin, that we might be made the righteousness of God in Him. In so doing He became the Mercy Seat that we might be invited and initiated as partakers and be invested to show forth the glory of God.

> There is a spot where spirits blend,
>   And friend holds fellowship with friend,
> A place than all beside, more sweet,
>   It is the bloodstained mercy seat.

THE MIGHTY GOD

His name shall be called Wonderful Counsellor, The mighty God (Isa. 9:6).

El Gibbor, which is rendered by the title *mighty God,* has in the word "mighty" the sense of being heroic, and has been so rendered by some "the God Hero." The clash of conflict, the clatter of strenuous opposition promoted by an obdurate oppressor, needs to be faced and fought, therefore the very character of the enemy calls for a champion with chivalrous courage to meet the onslaught. Christ is that heroic contestant who entered into a truceless warfare with the foe, to give battle wherever desired, not clad with military accouterments but with the whole armor of God, which includes the breastplate of righteousness and the sword of the Spirit. This same prophet in Isaiah 59:17-19 declares that this Redeemer would put on righteousness as a breastplate and adjust the helmet of salvation while at the same time the Spirit of the Lord would lift up a standard against the enemy.

The powers of darkness, which are referred to in the New Testament as the kingdom of darkness, are pictured at the close of the preceding chapter of Isaiah and the description is terrible to contemplate. To those driven to darkness and who as the result sat in darkness and the shadow of death, came the light of the Sun of righteousness (Isa. 9:2). How desperately man needed the mighty God with His heroic fortitude to intervene, the very Captain of our salvation to confront this diabolical power.

Ere Christ commenced His ministry of mercy among men, He went forth to meet the great adversary of truth and light, in the solitude of the wilderness, the place of no associates and no assistance and where no animated audience applauds and acclaims. He stood alone with the great accuser, the most subtle of all assailants, the worst enemy, the dread Apollyon. Verily He grappled with the fiend of falsity wherever he set the battle in array. Where would we look to find another who could face this deviser of deceit, this destroying devourer, and dictator of death?

The same is he who instigated the dreadful catalog of crime and who demanded as Goliath of old, that a man should come forth who would dare confront his sinister might and decide the issue in single combat.

Among the ranks of this world's warriors no one was found who could worthily uphold the honor of righteousness and truth. As the result the whole human race had been held in bondage for centuries by him who had the power of death. The same conditions pertained as in the days when the cruel Assyrian tyrant who gouged out eyes, split noses, and lopped off ears, invaded the land of Israel—none dared chirp [none peeped AV] (Isa. 10:14).

Suddenly an astonished inquirer asks, "Who *is* this, that cometh from Edom, with dyed garments from Bozrah that is glorious in His apparel, marching in the greatness of His strength?" And the answer rings out shrill and clear, "I that speak in righteousness, mighty to save" (Isa. 63:1). This exceptional description of the indefatigable Deliverer suddenly appearing in battle dress is one of the most thrilling sights to the soul of man, and recalls another august occasion when the same Conqueror approached the everlasting doors. "Who is this?" pealed across the azure leagues of space, and the ever-reverberating proclamation sounded through the heavens, "The LORD strong and mighty, the LORD mighty in battle" (Ps. 24:8). We read again of this Warrior as He advanced toward the field of conflict (Matt. 21:10).

> When the noblest battle that ever was fought,
>   And the greatest victory was won,
> Without a single comrade near
>   And without one shot from a gun.

The Lion of the tribe of Judah has prevailed, the mighty One has overcome the foe, the Son of man has triumphed gloriously. In the sacred splendor of Scripture symbolism, the Person of Christ and His manifold service are always the chief subject. If the proof of Christ's deity and godhead had been established in no other way, His great victory over the devil and death assures it forevermore.

This illustrious illuminator has flashed the light of the knowl-edge of salvation across the centuries so that those that sat in darkness and the shadow of death have seen a great light, the light of life.

As we contemplate the character of the conflict at issue, the caliber of the contestants involved, and the Champion whose complete conquest subjugated the foe forever, we are struck with the relevancy of the rendering "the God Hero," *El Gibbor*.

The expression graphically conveys one of the sterling and indispensable aspects of our Saviour's many-sided character. Mighty in this case means much more than authority, since it implies the replete resource to advance and attack the adver-sary, and the resolute chivalry and courage to overthrow the wicked one. The Prince of Peace is perfectly equipped with power to prevail, strength to subdue, and might to master every foe. Our Warrior Deliverer braved the fierce battle, broke the tyranny of the tempter, and in righteousness waged and won the war of the ages against wickedness. Of this portraiture of Christ as depicted in the Gospels from Matthew to John we may say, Behold! He is mighty in majesty, mighty in mastery, mighty in mercy, and mighty in ministry, therefore He is mighty to save, mighty to keep, and mighty to perfect for presentation before the presence of His glory with exceeding joy.

THE MESSIAH THE PRINCE

Know therefore and understand, that from the going forth of the commandment to restore and build Jerusalem unto Messiah the Prince shall be seven weeks and three score and two weeks. The street shall be built again and the wall even in troublous times, and after threescore and two weeks shall Messiah cut off both the city and the sanctuary that they shall be no more His (Dan. 9:25 Dr. George Faber's trans.)

Thirty-six other references to the Hebrew word *marsheeagh*, which is rendered anointed, occur in the Old Testament, but in these two instances the title Messiah appears. Therefore we know definitely that Messiah means the Anointed. A passage familiar to most readers is found in Psalm 2:2, "The kings of the earth set themselves, and rulers take counsel together, against the LORD, and against his anointed." The Spirit of God assures the identification in Acts 4:26-28.

The portion selected for our heading is one of the most profound prophecies of the Scriptures of truth, and Messiah, who is the main subject of the same, is the most preferable of princes, the most reliable of rulers, the most desirable of deliverers, the most amiable of authorities, the most laudable of liberators, and the most honorable in headship of the holy ones. His glorious name will one day be regarded and revered as excellent in all the earth (Ps. 8:1,9).

At this stage we are introduced to One who is wholly and absolutely approved of God, whose coming was announced for generations and whose aim as the Anointed of God was to fulfill the divine will and purpose completely and finally. Messiah is the Prince, a designation which describes His magnificent majesty and significant sovereignty. The title is used variously to disclose the widest range of administrative authority, wherefore He is called "the Prince of life" (Acts 3:15); "a Prince and a Saviour" (Acts 5:31); "the Prince of Peace" (Isa. 9:6); "the Prince of the kings of the earth" (Rev. 1:5); and the "Prince of princes" (Dan. 8:25). Therefore Christ is not only Prince in the sphere of material and physical majesty, but also in the realm of moral and spiritual mystery. The word mystery as used in the New Testament does not refer to that which is unknowable, but to that which can only be known through revelation and initiation. (Eph. 3:4-5,9).

Wherefore the advent of Messiah into the world, His anointing for identification, His reconciling death and astounding ascension to the right hand of God, furnish the hinges of history, the highlights of hope, and constitute the harbingers of heavenly glory. Why, may we ask, did not such a manifestation with its stupendous issues take place a millenium earlier? This matter was predetermined in the counsels of creation and redemption and graven into the plan of the eternal purpose to the effect that not until the fullness of time was reached would He appear (Gal. 4:4).

In His essential character He was ever Messiah, He ever was Mediator, but the day dawned in the history of mankind when these realities were made manifest. The relative prophecies were clear and explicit and when the appointed hour drew nigh, the tide of expectation ran high in Jerusalem. Aristobulus, a previous high priest, had been murdered at the instigation of Herod the Great for proclaiming the anticipated advent of Messiah the King as being at hand. Later, Herod's beautiful wife, with her family, suffered a similar fate, because Herod feared his eldest son, on attaining his majority, might become the acclaimed ruler of the Jews. When the wise men arrived in Jerusalem with their startling inquiry, Herod was troubled, for he seemed to think he had definitely trounced out of the mind of the community the possibility of such a thing ever being realized. Later he turned his attention to the center where he was informed Christ would arise and ordered the sword to sweep through the nurseries of Bethlehem until all the little feet of the male children were stiffened, and trotted no more on the overhead floor. But no dictatorial monarch, no matter how determined he might be, could ever frustrate the fulfillment of a divine purpose, purposed in Christ Jesus before the world began.

Aged Simeon, the discerner who waited for the consolation of Israel, recognized the true character of the child (Luke 2:28-29). Anna, the devout soul who spoke to all who looked for a redemption in Israel, had a clear understanding of the times. Yea, and in Samaria a delinquent who had known brighter days gave expression to the words, "We know that Messiah cometh which is called Christ" (John 4:25). The knowledge of His anticipated appearance was widespread.

Messiah held for centuries a particular and peculiar relationship toward Jerusalem with its people, and to the Temple with its priesthood. All through that period He had attracted affections and awakened pulsations of love that were felt in Heaven. The ancient covenant had been ratified as a solemn compact of agreement, Israel had plighted fidelity and promised obedience, but the regrettable history as a whole is stated by Stephen in Acts 7:52-53. Now the hour had struck for the terminating of the old bonds that had concluded the covenant (Ex. 19:8).

"After threescore and two weeks shall Messiah cut off both the city and the sanctuary that they shall be no more His." Zechariah had predicted this grave enactment. "And I took my staff, even Beauty, and cut it asunder, that I might break my covenant which I had made with all the people. And it was broken in that day: and so the poor of the flock that waited upon me knew that it was the word of the LORD" (Zech. 11:10-11). The verses that follow identify these things as taking place during the manifestation and ministry of Messiah. Zechariah declared earlier in his message that the symbol of divine glory which was withheld from the second temple would come in substance to the very house Zerubbabel was building (Zech. 2:5; 4:6-7). Haggai confirmed this (Hag. 2:9), while Malachi corroborated the same (Mal. 3:1). If Messiah did not come to the Temple Zerubbabel rebuilt as He promised, He never can and never will, for it was destroyed well nigh nineteen centuries ago.

Both Dr. George Faber and Sir Isaac Newton point out that the verb used in Daniel 9:26 is not passive but active voice, and therefore the cutting off is not something done to Christ, but something that He does. Dr. B. Blaney wholly endorses this fact. The works of these three scholarly and devout men were published prior to the erroneous writings of Rabbi Ben Ezra, so called, which appeared in print in 1808, and which have so grievously corrupted protestant teaching on prophecy, the very thing it was designed to do. History verifies the translation herein used, for Messiah disowned His people and discarded the Temple, even to predicting its desolation. This action constituted the great divorcement. Isaiah predicted that the leaders of the nation would one day complain of the treatment received at the hand of the Lord, and that He would say, "Where is the bill of your mother's divorcement, whom I have put away?" (Isa. 50:1)

The cause is then stated in the verses that follow, and Messiah describes the treatment He received at the nation's hands, the personal pronouns I, My, Mine, and Me being used thirty-four times in verses 1-9. He who as Creator hides the heavens in blackness (verse 3), later, when acting as the covenant-breaker bearing iniquity, hid not His face from shame and spitting (verse 6). For the legal aspect of these matters, the thirtieth chapter of Numbers should be carefully studied. The view given of Israel as a daughter in subjection, as a wife in submission, as a widow sorrow-stricken, and as a divorced woman in separation, forms the subject of its contents. If, after hearing the vow, it be allowed to stand, as was the case of Israel's vow at Sinai, and the Lord should, at some later date disallow the vow, "then He shall bear her iniquity" (Num. 30:15).

Numbers 30 foreshadows Christ disanulling Israel's promise and ratification of the covenant. During the manifestation He actually disallowed the nation's vow by saying, "Moses gave you the law and none of you keepeth the law" (John 7:19; see Zech. 11:10). Numbers 30 also forecasts His bearing Israel's penalty for iniquity (verse 15). "Thou hast cast off and abhorred, Thou hast been wroth with Thine anointed. Thou hast made void the covenant of Thy servant" (Ps. 89:38-39). Yea, the portion foretells His fulfilling Israel's pledge and resolution. This fact is repeatedly confirmed in Scripture: "I will pay my vows before them that fear Him" (Ps. 22:25); "He will magnify the law, and make it honourable" (Isa. 42:21). Furthermore Numbers 30 foresees Christ securing Israel's peace and reconciliation (verses 5,8,12), "the Lord shall forgive." Therefore the redeemed say, "The chastisement of our peace was upon Him."

This phase of Messiah's suffering and sacrifice follows the divorcement and is graphically portrayed in Isaiah 53. Herein is stated the recognition of what has transpired. "Surely He hath borne *our* griefs, and carried *our* sorrows. . . . He was wounded for *our* transgressions, He was bruised for *our* iniquities: the chastisement of *our* peace was upon Him; and with His stripes we are healed" (Isa. 53:4-5). Attention should be drawn to the fact that in this section of Isaiah's message, Israel is referred to as daughter (52:2), wife (54:6), widow (54:4), and a woman forsaken (54:6), while Christ is referred to as Husband (54:5) in confirmation of the relationships portrayed in Numbers 30.

The importance of these matters cannot be overestimated, and by virtue of being overlooked, they constitute the crux of the cause of the confusion in prophetic interpretation in the past. Dr. Faber points out another significant fact in connection with the fourth feature of Daniel 9:24, which he renders "to bring in the everlasting righteous one," or "the Righteous One of the everlasting ages." Righteousness is not a standard but a person, "the Lord our righteouness," the One whose ways have been from of old, from everlasting (Mic. 5:2). In this light, the question of John, "Art Thou He that should come?" is perfectly revelant.

Let us reconsider the glorious merits and gracious meekness which combine the mission and ministry of Messiah the Prince, whose sovereign eye surveys the universal situation at all times and whose supreme hand sways the unrivaled scepter of all power in Heaven and on earth.

The strength of the vital claims He made was confirmed by the very character of the death He died, which was at one and the same time virtuous, vicarious, and victorious.

THE MEDIATOR

For there is one God, and one mediator between God and men, the man Christ Jesus; Who gave Himself a ransom for all (1 Tim. 2:5-6).

Now a mediator is not a mediator of one, but God is one (Gal. 3:20).

One of the grandest and most distinctive doctrines of the gospel is the declaration of one God and one Mediator. The glorious message of salvation has been greatly simplified by virtue of these two vital facts. The word "mediator" is a New Testament title and refers to one who stands in the midst of two parties who are out of accord with each other, as with the intent of reinstating harmony through reconciliation. The function is graphically stated by Job when he says, "For He is not a man, as I am, that I should answer Him, and we should come together in judgment. Neither is there any daysman betwixt us, that might lay his hand upon us both" (Job 9:32-33). Man is vividly conscious that the many devious means he devises in order to meet the demands of a just God against sin are altogether unavailing. Therefore, the plaintive appeal of the human heart for an advocate to mediate is age-old and worldwide. This accounts for the records of peoples and nations throughout eastern lands lionizing their ethnic mediators who have been held up as the hope of the helpless, such as Buddha, Krishna, Zoroaster, and Confucius.

A true mediator must be free of all prejudice and partiality, and possessed of a character that is flawless and faultless. Moreover, he must be available everywhere and always, and accessible to everyone at all times. The function cannot be discharged without a full knowledge of all languages and dialects of every race, caste, and clime. Omniscience is the first qualification, and to be available and accessible to everyone everywhere requires omnipresence. Futhermore, in order to be in a position to undertake for the needs of mankind universally, onmipotence is essential. These three attributes, as we term them, for they are actually indescribable qualities, constitute the indispensable requisites of a Mediator, and the Scripture affirms there is but one, the Man Christ Jesus.

Such a spacious ministry as mediation entails makes the office superhuman and supernatural, for it involves standing between deity and humanity. Herein the highest honors and stateliest splendors rest upon the only-begotten of the Father. We may visualize Christ as the One equal with the Most High, as the Son of God, or view Him in manifestation on the human level as the

Son of man, and we shall search in vain for another possessed of characteristics such as these which are so absolutely essential in mediation.

The more we meditate upon this majestic Mediator, who is so mighty and yet so meek, so matchless and yet so merciful, the more we become convinced of His suitability to fulfill all the obligations that devolve upon so sacred an office. We at once recognize that the supremacy of His might is perfectly balanced by the sublimity of His mercy and we realize that His ponderous power is in complete harmony with His precious pity. Yea, as declared to Job, "Behold God is mighty and despiseth not any." He is too sublime to be suspicious, He is too consistent to be contemptuous, He is too sympathetic to be censorious, and He is too considerate to be capricious. He does not despise a single soul, but calmly and correctly administers judgment or assures justification as the case requires. The ages themselves can in no wise erase one atom of effectiveness from His advocacy, because He ever liveth to make intercession for His people.

Sir John Alexander Clarke, who was knighted by the late King Albert of Belgium in acknowledgment of his missionary states-manship in the Belgian Congo, tells a remarkable story of medi-ative advocacy which aptly illustrates one phase of our Saviour's work.

He had completed the translation of the New Testament into the Kiluba language, but was far from satisfied with the word he had used to convey the idea of advocate. "We have an advocate with the Father, Jesus Christ the righteous" (1 John 2:1). His quest for a more suitable word than *sangu,* which implied comforter, and referred to a mother's breast in relation to her child, continued for over two years. The day arrived when he reached the capital city of the Mulongo territory, and the king, hearing of the white man's arrival, came out to meet him clad in beautiful leopard skins. After a friendly greeting Sir John was es-corted to the king's residence and while he was seated in the throne room a significant-looking character entered, and after receiving his orders for the day, departed. When he had left the room the king referred to him as Nsenga Mukwashi, and Sir John asked, "What did you say was his name?"

The king repeated the words and added, "That is not his name, but his office." "Then what does he do?" was the eager inquiry. The answer was of much interest to the missionary.

"As you know, I am a great king and am anxious to see that justice is done for all my people. The cases requiring attention are too numerous for me to listen to by myself, so my Nsenga Mukwashi does the interviewing and presents concisely the main facts of the case to me, and I give my verdict and issue a decision."

"May I go to the outpost at the entrance of the city and see him at work?" asked the missionary.

"You are quite free to do," answered the king. So Sir John arose and was given an escort to take him to the lookout station, from whence it was possible to scan the vast open spaces of the veldt. After a brief conversation the advocate said, "Three women are coming, one is old, the two younger are accompanying her." Sir John thought his sight was good, but when he placed his hand above his eyes to peer across the plain, he could see what appeared to be three dots in the far distance, but it was utterly impossible to determine whether they were men or women. Then the advocate said he would set out to meet them and would hear and know the case by the time they arrived at the city limits. When they drew near Sir John saw with the king's representative an elderly woman and two younger women. On reaching the city entrance the group started to return to the royal residence. While enroute the elderly woman said to the official, "Where are you taking me?"

"I am taking you to meet the great king," said he.

"Do not do that," she replied.

"Why not?"

"Because I am old and timid and would become speechless in the king's presence."

"There will be no need for you to speak," said he, "I have heard the whole matter and I shall speak for you." On arrival at the palace they entered the throne room. The king immediately turned his attention to his advocate, who briefly explained the case. The husband of the old woman had died and three of the neighbors were endeavoring to wrest the compound from the widow and eject her from the hut. After hearing the report, the king's eyes flashed a fiery glance and he commanded the widow and her companions to be cared for, and after a day's rest, to be escorted back to their village with necessary provisions for the three days' journey. He also ordered a group of guards to go to the scene, arrest the culprits, and bring them to the capital for sentence.

Sir John said it was worth waiting the two years to see enacted so dramatically the very task of advocacy for which he had sought an apt word to use in his translation of the New Testament.

Let us be mindful that we have an Advocate with the Father eternal, One who is a faithful Friend and who fully knows our cause and is perfectly able to protect our highest interests, preserve us from a haughty foe, and provide adequately the help we need.

THE MESSENGER OF THE COVENANT

> Behold, I will send My messenger, and He shall prepare the way before Me: and the Lord, whom ye seek, shall suddenly come to His temple, even the messenger of the covenant, whom ye delight in (Mal. 3:1)

The congenial figure of Christ as the Messenger assures us of God's definite interest in man. The fact that Christ assumes this feature expresses the reality of His love toward us, while the function He thus adopts clearly announces the Father's special favor toward mankind in sending such an envoy. The Apostle John affirms that the Father sent the Son to be the Saviour of the world (1 John 4:14). Wherefore Christ appeared as God's Messenger of mercy, His heavenly Herald of hope, and His regal Representative to repeal the old agreement with Israel and ratify the new covenant. In view of so significant a commission, He was required to hold the highest credentials, and these were not only evidenced, but confirmed by His superior character and sterling conduct. If any should demand evidential proof to verify the distinguished rank Christ holds in this province, we would say, "The Spirit is the stateliest teacher, the Bible is the standard token, the Church is the strongest testimony, and the Jew is the specified touchstone to confirm that He came as the Messenger of the covenant."

His deeds of devotion delightfully charmed the Father's heart. His words of wisdom were welcome music to eternal ears. His love and loveliness fascinated the angelic hosts. His honor and holiness thrilled the ranks of cherubim and seraphim. From this sphere of supernal society He came as Messenger to confirm the covenant, to mediate for man, to make known the mercy of the Almighty, and to manifest immortal life.

The words Christ spoke bore the celestial stamp of divine authorship, while His works wore the special marks of divine authority.

So dignified a messenger as He, deigning to traverse so great a distance in the service of deity, most surely warrants our expecting Him to bring a wonderful message, containing the brightest designs and most blessed decrees that were ever dispatched from the throne above. Certainly the message would contain the wisest and most winsome news that was ever published and would include the widest conceivable range of benefits for all who were willing to receive the Messenger. We conclude also that we are right in declaring that it would be disastrous and damaging for any soul to despise the dignity of the Bearer of such tidings, or to deny Him a hearing. What an inscrutable moral mystery is presented in this matter. How strange it appears that everyone's attention is not arrested and amazed at the presence of such a delegate, for His ways are otherworldly, His courtesies belong to a heavenly country, and His character indicates He is an ambassador from a celestial court. His purpose in coming from the confines of eternity was to communicate the immutable counsels of the city of God, and for the establishment of His everlasting covenant.

With a dauntless courage and defectless courtesy He presented His credentials to the rulers of Israel but was coldly and critically received. Yet the fact remains that neither in the whole range of revelation, nor throughout the entire realm of redemption, is there anyone who can in any wise compare with this precious, gracious, wondrous Messenger.

A flood of light is thrown upon the function of this representative in the book of Job where we read, "If there be a messenger
with Him, an interpreter, one among a thousand, to show unto
man his uprightness: then He is gracious unto him and saith,
Deliver him from going down to the pit, I have found a ransom"
(Job 33:23-24). So the Messenger is also the Interpreter of God's
uprightness in all His dealings with mankind. We need only to
examine His message on law, which is the most searching ever
delivered, His message on love, which is the most satisfying ever
disclosed, His message on life, which is the most stimulating ever
divulged, and His message on light, which is the most startling
ever declared, if we require convincing on the subject.

With these surpassing features we should consider the interpretation He brings of the moral law, the illustration He gives
of divine love, the instruction He supplies on eternal life, and
the illumination He sheds on the source and summit of the light
of knowledge. The truth He taught on such themes transcends
all previous instruction that was ever given anywhere by anyone. He never once shelved the truth to serve the hour, nor at
any time catered for display in seeking power. Truly Christ is
the Messenger of the covenant.

> We've a message to give to the nations
> That the Lord who reigneth above
> Has sent us His son to save us
> And show us that God is love.
> C. STERNE

Over two hundred references occur in the Old Testament in
which the word "messenger" is used. Three times it is rendered
"ambassadors," and ninety-six times the "angel" of the covenant or "Angel of the Lord." Because the nature of the message
was so vitally important, the most venerable of all Heaven was
sent to deliver it to mankind.

THE MASTER

The Master is come, and calleth for thee (John 11:28).
Ye call me Master and Lord: and ye say well; for so I am (John 13:13).

In the prolific returns of treasure derived from the study of Christ's names and titles, those which He Himself advanced contribute the greater pleasure and profit. From among these we now select the instructive designation, Master. We do not wish to intrude a lesson on Greek substantives but merely introduce five of the Greek words that are rendered in our English version master, in order to comprehend a little more of the personal rights and claims of our blessed Saviour.

The chief word is *kurios,* which our Lord used when He said, "No man can serve two masters" (Matt. 6:24). The title implies claim, right, and ownership and in this case of its use, shows us that He holds the supreme claim, the sole right, and the singular ownership. The inner meaning indicates purchase right because of the price He paid to secure His people, in the light of which the Apostle Paul, when addressing the body of believers at Corinth stated, "ye are not your own; for ye are bought with a price" (1 Cor. 6:19-20; 7:23). The gallant British officer Captain Hedley Vicars was reading this portion in his tent before dawn on the battlefield of Crimea on March 22, 1854. He was arrested at the thought, "Ye are not your own." "We cannot use as we like that which is not our own," said he, and knelt to re-dedicate his life to the service of his rightful owner. We cannot spend our time, strength, and resources as we please if we own His purchase right. If we believe we are His we must behave accordingly.

The second word is *didaskolos.* "She turned herself, and saith unto Him, Rabboni; which is to say, Master" (John 20:16). The fifty-eight occurrences of this word in the New Testament indicate that Christ is the instructor, teacher, and disciplinarian who trains and tutors His followers in the knowledge of God and spiritual truth for their perfecting. His great design is not to fill the head with learning, but to flood the heart with love, that we might become examples, expressions, and exponents of His teaching. Our English word is derived from *didatic,* to teach.

The third word is *kathegetes.* "One is your Master" (Matt. 23:8). In this instance the Lord is the Leader, the Example, and the Guide. If we be considered the sheep of His flock, He is our leader as the Shepherd; if we are saints in His church, He is our example as Sanctifier; if we are serving as stewards, He is our overseer as Guide. "I am among you as one that serveth," said He, "if any would be great among you let him become servant to all." If we submit and obey He will add dignity to the life, purity to the heart, integrity to the soul, and wisdom to the speech. Moreover, He will use us for some task that will bring honor to His name and help to our neighbors.

The fourth word is *epistates,* a title confined to the Gospel of Luke, in which it is used seven times. Said Peter, "Master, we have toiled all the night, and have taken nothing" (Luke 5:5). In this case the name means estimator, valuer, appraiser, and Peter is eager to have the Lord express His estimate on work that has seemed so unprofitable. When told to launch out and let down the nets he implies, "What is the use, we have toiled the whole night through without avail. Would you have us add deeper disgust to our present disappointment?" The Appraiser desired to remunerate Peter for the use of his boat which He had borrowed while He taught the multitude. The partial obedience of Peter in letting down one net only was the cause of losing part of the haul, but as the outcome, the disciples learned that the Master had better judgment than they. The estimate placed upon Peter's willingness to lend his boat for two or three hours, even when he was tired, was to Christ worth a whole boatload of fish. This Valuer never permits anyone to intrude in His province, in giving an estimate of the value of work that is done for Him. He reserves to Himself the sole right. When Judas tried to butt in on one occasion, he was sternly rebuked (John 12:4-8).

Our fifth title for master is *despotes,* from which we derive the word despot. Paul said to Timothy, "If a man therefore purge himself from these, he shall be a vessel unto honour, sanctified, and meet for the master's use, and prepared unto every good work" (2 Tim. 2:21). The ten occurrences of this word are of deep interest and the meaning signifies monarch, autocrat, or despot, and refers to one who has supreme possession and will not brook any rival claimant to a single vestige of what He owns. The relationship is not one into which I must enter, but I may. The magnificent bearing of this Master, His miraculous power, and marvelous wisdom are all swayed by the magistracy of His matchless love. The picture is taken from the metaphor of the potter who has a bright and beautiful design in mind for common clay, to mold it into vessels of utility and dignity. What does it mean to have the high honor of becoming a prized vessel possessed and protected by such an owner, belonging to a personage of such caliber, the Master of multitudes? This is He who at once is the Purchaser with sole right, the Perfecter with one aim, the Pattern with clearest type, the Proprietor with purest motive, and the Possessor with total claim.

THE MINISTER OF THE SANCTUARY

Now of the things which we have spoken this is the sum: We have such an high priest, who is set on the right hand of the throne of the Majesty in the heavens; A minister of the sanctuary, and of the true tabernacle, which the Lord pitched, and not man (Heb. 8:1-2).

Numerous references in the Scriptures speak of Christ as discharging the official function of a minister. He taught His disciples that as Son of man He came not to be ministered unto but to minister.

The Apostle Paul declared that Jesus Christ became a minister of the circumcision for the truth of God to confirm the promises made to the fathers (Rom. 15:8). These aspects were linked with our Lord's ministry on earth, but in the present instance He is depicted as a Minister of the heavenly sanctuary to dispense the blessings and distribute the benefits secured by virtue of His being the Mediator of the new covenant. This conspicuous and continuous service is spoken of as His more excellent ministry (Heb. 8:6).

We have already considered His mercy as the Mighty One which is so munificent, the mission of His Messiahship, which is so memorable, the merit of His Mediatorship, which is so magnificent, His message as the Messenger of the covenant which is so matchless, the majesty of His Mastership which is so magnanimous and here we come to His ministration as Minister of the celestial sanctuary, a ministry that is manifold and measureless in both its resource and range. In the exercise of this official capacity He bestows the maximum of blessing on millions of the redeemed eternally. Therefore the title expands the magnitude of Christ's priestly ministry of maintenance to a degree of immortality that is immeasurable and infinite.

We should always bear in mind that this glorious ministry Christ maintains as High Priest is after the order of Melchisedec, whose main function was to refresh and renew with divine blessing, in the name of the Most High, possessor of Heaven and earth. Abraham received this benediction (Gen. 14:19-20), wherefore all the nations of the earth are blessed as the result (Gen. 18:18). The faith of Abraham which is personal is frequently dealt with, but the blessing of Abraham which is universal is seldom touched upon. That blessing is still being ministered by virtue of the priestly ministration of Christ which is after the order of Melchisedec, as so clearly set forth in the Gospel of Luke. Another graphic illustration of our Lord's lofty status and vital service is also supplied from the same book of Genesis. After Joseph had secured and stored the sustantial sufficiencies of Egyptian produce, he was made minister of supplies in the whole country, to administer the bounty he had gathered. Pharaoh committed everything into his hands and made him sole distributor. The Son of man secured far greater advantages and privileges in the realms invisible, for the Father hath given all things into His hands (John 13:3). Wherefore the Church is blessed with all spiritual blessings in the heavenlies in Christ.

Following His ascension to the right hand of the Majesty on high, He gave gifts unto men (Eph. 4:8). Among these were the gift of eternal life (Rom. 6:23), the gift of righteousness (Rom. 5:17), the gift of salvation (Eph. 2:8), the gift of His Holy Spirit and many more. The blessings likewise He ministers are inestimable and consist of salvation, sanctification, sustentation, redemption, reconciliation, regeneration, remission, emancipation, and justification, together with deliverance, acceptance, and recompense. Yea, He is the One who perfumes our praise, provides our peace, and perfects our prayers. Each of these ceaseless ministries is carried on through the centuries on behalf of a great concourse of countless millions of souls. This constitutes one of the greatest marvels of Christ's mediative ministry revealed in the Scriptures.

In this superior station the High Priest is attended by a vast retinue of angels. The Prophet Daniel describes a scene in which millions ministered unto Him (Dan. 7:10). The Apostle John confirmed this witness and verified the fact by giving us a specific statement that one hundred million angels were in attendance, and then he plunged into the sphere of the indefinite by saying, "and thousands of thousands" (Rev. 5:11). A thousand thousand is one million, and in this case with the use of the plural he purposely intends a figurative number that is beyond the bounds of human calculation, or to use the later statement, "a great host that no man can number" (Rev. 7:9). In the book from whence our title is taken we are told that the angels are ministering spirits, sent forth to minister to those who are heirs of salvation. So then we may state correctly that our Lord and Saviour is the Minister of ministers.

First, He has all the supernatural *credentials* that are necessary to be able to minister, in which capacity no other celebrity could possibly qualify. These indispensable requisites include the mysteries of omniscience, the majesties of omnipotence, and the mercies of omnipresence. This assures us that with perfect knowledge of all things mysterious and manifest, with perfect power in the visible and invisible realms and with a perfect love which is sovereign and sympathetic both in Heaven and earth, He is adequately able to minister fully and unfailingly on behalf of everyone.

Secondly, He also has the superhuman *essentials* that are required in order to be the Minister of the celestial sanctuary of the heavens. From among these we may make mention of the sanctity of His high honor, the suitability of His holiness, and the sympathy of His heart. Each of these features was clearly verified during the manifestation. As the Son, He fully honored the Father and the Father frankly honored Him. He fervently challenged His severest critics to disprove His sinlessness, but without response, and He gratuitously described for us the graces of His wondrous heart of compassion. What a blessed assurance it is to know that we are accepted in the Beloved!

Thirdly, He holds the control of superlative *potentials* apart from which ministering proficiently and perennially would be utterly impossible. For brevity's sake we shall menton but three of these faculties, His freshness, His fullness, and His faithfulness. His freshness is age-abiding, for He has the dew of His youth from the womb of the morning (Ps. 110:3). The holy vitality of His vigor and virtue are immune from all taint of staleness or tinge of weariness (Isa. 40:28). Therefore His fullness is likened in the symbols of Scripture to a star ever scintillating, a sun ever shining, a fountain ever flowing, a blossom ever blooming, a lover ever loving, a ruler ever reigning, a shepherd ever sustaining, and a light everlasting, so that we are filled full in Him. In relation to His faithfulness, how shall we utter it? Said David, "Thy faithfulness reacheth unto the skies" (Ps. 36:5). The AV has "clouds," but it is the same word as in Psalm 18:11. The prophet Jeremiah stated, "Great is Thy faithfulness" (Lam. 3:23), so of this attribute we are absolutely confident. As minister of the heavenly sanctuary Christ by far outmatches in rank and outvies in riches the grandest of the great, the mightiest of the strong, and the holiest of the true. He may be approached through prayer, and He taught at the close of His earthly ministry, in the strongest terms and simplest language, the precious privileges and priceless possibilities available to those who ask, seek, and knock through the medium of sincere prayer.

There is an eye that never sleeps beneath the wing of night.
There is an ear that never shuts, when sink the
    beams of light.
There is an arm that never tires when human strength
    gives way,
There is a love that never fails when earthly loves decay.
That eye is fixed on sereph throngs, that arm upholds the sky,
That ear is filled with heavenly songs, that love is
    throned on high.
There is a power that faith can wield, when mortal aid is vain,
That eye, that arm, that love to reach, that listening
    ear to gain.
That power is prayer which soars above, to Jesus on the throne,
And moves the hand that rules the world, to bring
    deliverance down.

THE MAINTAINER

Preserve me, O God: for in Thee do I put my trust.... The Lord is the portion of mine inheritance and of my cup: Thou maintainest my lot. The lines are fallen unto me in pleasant places; yea, I have a goodly heritage (Ps. 16:1,5-6).

The words "maintain," "maintenance," and "maintaineth" occur ten times in the Old Testament and their derivation con-tributes a wide variety of meaning which is applied to one of the dignified capacities of Christ in His important office as custodian of His people's rights. Ere His function began in this relation-ship, He stooped from being in the form of God and took on Him the form of a servant, and being found in fashion as a man, He humbled Himself and became obedient unto death, where-fore He has been highly exalted. His confidence in the Father, who maintained the Son's rights while and when He endured the avalanche of agony and reproach, comes first, and leads us on to the latter aspect in which He who was maintained becomes the Maintainer. Peter uses the former application of the figure as it pertains to Christ, in His being upheld during those terrible hours immediately preceding His death (Acts 2:26-28). If we turn a moment to the prophets we find this interpretation fully substantiated. "Behold My servant, whom I uphold. . . . Fear thou not; for I am with thee: be not dismayed; for I am thy God: I will strengthen thee; yea, I will help thee; yea, I will uphold thee with the right hand of My righteousness" (Isa. 42:1; 41:10).

The word rendered uphold in these two instances is the same as that rendered maintaineth in other instances. Christ was upheld by the Father during His crucial ordeal when He submitted in sacrifice amid an atmosphere of terrible pressure and devilish persecution. What a paradox, that this One who in His manhood needed to be upheld in His abysmal grief, is nevertheless the One who in His godhead is "upholding all things by the word of His power" (Heb. 1:3).

In other words, the Man of Sorrows, in the day of His crucifixion, becomes the Man of Sovereignty in the hour of His coronation at the right hand of the Majesty in the heavens. The theme sustained throughout Psalm 16 is the contentment derived from a conspicuous confidence, and as we are told elsewhere, "Godliness with contentment is great gain." How encouraging and heartening it becomes to envisage this great Emancipator of the flock as being the Maintainer of our inheritance. Who is more able than the Ancient of Days to do this? No pretentious usurper has any room to dispute or deny our Lord's ability to protect the interests of His beloved people. We may recall that when Joshua divided the land among the tribes of Israel Levi was not listed, his service was in the sanctuary, therefore the Lord said, "I am thine inheritance." The terms used here, such as cup, lot, lines, and heritage, bespeak the circumstances associated with that far-off occasion, but Joshua did not survive the stroke of death and was rendered incompetent to uphold the rights he had secured. We possess a permanent Protector to safeguard our securities, for the heavenly

treasures of the true believer which are described as unsearchable riches, and riches in glory, are altogether outside of the
range of moth or rust to corrupt and beyond the boundary of
thieves to steal.

When the Son of man opened a door of deliverance to the
enslaved of earth, He swung wide the portal of peace to the
emancipated and paved the highway to the gates of glory, so
that His enlightened people might enter into everlasting habitations and possess their possessions. He who is the Mainspring
of creation also became Magister of the Church and is abundantly competent to defend every right, title, and claim which He
secured on behalf of the redeemed.

These securities include the privileges of sonship, the possessions of heirship, the pleasures of fellowship, the powers of
kingship, the promises of citizenship, the principles of partner-
ship, the potentials of judgeship, together with all the remaining
characteristics which pertain to the inheritance of the saints in
light.

This glorious Custodian of the heritage and heirship of God's
people is wholly worthy of the fervent confidence, firm reliance,
and full dependence of all the faithful who have reposed trust
in God. The final perseverance of the Prevailer for our preservation is definitely assured. He will continue to prosecute His
eternal purpose and perfect that which concerneth us until all
is finally consummated, and we receive and revel in the enduring substance of an eternal inheritance which is incorruptible,
undefiled, and unfading.

> Sing we of the golden city, pictured in the vision old,
> Everlasting light shines o'er it, wondrous things of it are told;
> Only righteous men and women, dwell within its jasper walls,
> Sin is banished from its borders, justice reigns in all its halls.

THE MAN CHRIST JESUS

For there is one God, and one mediator between God and men, the man Christ Jesus (1 Tim. 2:5).

If it were possible to find in the universe one perfect specimen of manhood, we would at once see the living expression of godhead, for God made man in His own image and likeness. This is exactly what we meet with in the Man Christ Jesus, who is Emmanuel, God with us. Intellectually, volitionally, and emotionally Christ is a complete man, although in mind, will, and heart He exemplified deity as well. No other person before or since has been able to stand on a plane of equality with Him. In the matter of persuasive oratory, "Never man spake like this man" (John 7:46). As far as omnipotence is concerned, "no man can do these miracles that Thou doest, except God be with him" (John 3:2), and again, "Behold the man, He shall build My temple, yea, He shall build My temple" (Zech. 6:12-13). His omniscience is also indicated, "Come, see a man, which told me all things that ever I did: is not this the Christ?" (John 4:29) Nor are the suggestions of His omnipresence lacking: "Sir, I have no man, when the water is troubled, to put me into the pool" (John 5:7), but Jesus is always available and able to do far more for the helpless and harassed (John 20:19,26).

This Man is conspicuously unique in His character and conduct (John 9:31,33), most comprehensive in His understanding (John 2:24), and certainly unsurpassed in beauty and glory (John 1:14). In the dignity of His manhood He is most excellent as the Son of man (Ps. 8:1), in the desirability of His saviourhood He is most resplendent as the Saviour of the world (John 4:42), and in the durability of His priesthood He is altogether efficient and able to save to the uttermost (Heb. 7:25). How worthy He is of the words of the hymn by M. P. Ferguson:

> Fairest of all the earth beside,
> Chiefest of all unto Thy bride,

Fullness divine in Thee I see,
Wonderful Man of Calvary.

Granting the sinner life and peace
Granting the captive sweet release
Shedding His blood to make us free,
Merciful Man of Calvary!

When the prophet Ezekiel witnessed a vision of glory that was transportingly rapturous, he described what he saw in the midst of the immortal splendor. "And above the firmament that was over their heads was the likeness of a throne, as the appearance of a sapphire stone: and upon the likeness of the throne was the likeness as the appearance of a man above upon it" (Ezek. 1:26). Solely because this Man brought the celestial realities from above into the realm of the terrestrial world below and overcame the infernal foe, could infinite glory and absolute security be vouch-safed to mankind. The disciples, in witnessing the magnificent display at the time of the transfiguration, when the two out-standing men of the old economy faded from view, "saw no man, save Jesus only" (Matt. 17:8).

Numerous reasons are given in Scripture for Christ becoming man in manifestation, and from among these we shall select six that are the most familiar, for the figure six is the number of man.

First, He became man in order to substantiate His right to redeem mankind. According to the Law of Moses it was essen-tial to be near of kin to be qualified to redeem. The Old Testa-ment law of redemption was clear and explicit, and no stranger or alien was permitted to attempt it. Wherefore Christ came into the world as Son of man to secure the legal right to redeem man. As Creator, or as Son of God, He did not hold a qualified relationship to become the Redeemer of Israel and Reconciler of the world.

Boaz, the mighty man of wealth in Bethlehem, undertook to redeem Ruth on the sole ground that according to law he was near of kin, and was both able and willing to act on her behalf.

In the second place Christ became man to be in a position to stipulate His qualifications when confronting the devil, whose decree of death had been passed upon all men, for all had sinned. "By one man sin entered into the world . . . wherefore the grace of God and the gift by grace is by one man Jesus Christ" (Rom. 5:12,15). The great enemy who held the power of death over mankind made an attempt in the first round of the temptation to persuade Christ into disqualifying Himself by performing an act that would demonstrate His deity. The devil said to Him, "If Thou be the Son of God command this stone that it be made bread." The reply Christ gave is sublime, "It is written, that *man* shall not live by bread alone, but by every word of God" (Luke 4:3).

This is as much as saying, "In that your decree of death is passed over all men I have become man to contest the strength of your power, and in My present capacity I hold the rightful, lawful privilege of challenging your authority."

In the third place, Christ became man as a solicitant to solicit man's interest and attract his attention as the available Deliverer from the bondage of death. His appeals were full of assurance. "Come unto Me, all ye that labour and are heavy laden, and I will give you rest" (Matt. 11:28). On the occasion when the officers of the temple court were sent to arrest Him, they heard Him proclaim in clear, ringing tones, "If any man thirst, let him come unto Me and drink," which intimates that "whoever thirsts for deliverance from bondage, longs for freedom, or desires satisfaction, let him come to Me." The deputation returned to their superiors who asked, "Why have ye not brought Him?" to which they replied: "Never man spake like this man" (John 7:46). Never before in history, nor since, has anyone appealed to man for faith, belief, and trust, who held out such amazing assurances of abiding satisfaction for all time and eternity as this Speaker did. A full release from distress, the devil, and death was guaranteed.

Fourthly, He became man to sublimate the status of humanity, heighten its dignity, and lift man into a new relationship by regeneration. "The first man is of the earth, earthy: the second man is the Lord from heaven.... And as we have borne the image of the earthy, we shall also bear the image of the heavenly" (1 Cor. 15:47,49). Said Nicodemus, the ruler in Israel, "No man can do these miracles that Thou doest, except God be with him." Jesus answered, "Except a man be born again, he cannot see the kingdom of God" (John 3:2,3). Following a new birth, the requirements for growth and development are supplied. The necessary instruction is furnished for well-being: "Till we all come in the unity of the faith, and of the knowledge of the Son of God, unto a perfect man, unto the measure of the stature of the fulness of Christ" (Eph. 4:13).

Fifthly, He became man to substitute His perfect life in man's stead, "in order to taste death for every man" (Heb. 2:9). "Forasmuch then as the children are partakers of flesh and blood, He also Himself likewise took part of the same; that through death He might destroy him who had the power of death, that is, the devil; and deliver them who through fear of death were all their lifetime subject to bondage" (Heb. 2:14-15). The verse that follows affirms that He did not adopt the nature of angels. Such a status would not have qualified Him to redeem man. This aspect is stated superlatively elsewhere: "Who, being in the form of God thought not equality with God a thing to be held tenaciously, but made Himself of no reputation, and took upon Him the form of a servant, and was made in the likeness of men. And being found in fashion as a man, He humbled Himself, and became obedient unto death, even the death of the cross" (Phil. 2:6-9 RV).

Sixthly, He became man in order to supplicate as a mediator between God and man. The man Christ Jesus has obtained a more excellent ministry than the service in which the Aaronic order functioned. He is the Mediator of a better covenant which is established upon better promises (Heb. 8:6).

> Behold the man the Christ uplifted high
> 'Twas for our sakes He came to earth to die.

And now He mediates with God above,
To prove the strength of His abiding love

Appointed priest adorned in robes of light,
He sits enthroned, assures to us our right;
We may approach, behold His glorious face,
And trace the marvels of His matchless grace.

N

The priceless values of Christ's perfect virtue, which were presented in His vicarious sacrifice, have added perpetual renown to His Name and glorious fame.

The NAME ABOVE EVERY NAME (Phil. 2:6-9)
> Our Lord's transcendent title of Truth and Triumph.

The NEAR OF KIN (Ruth 2:20; Sam. 19:42)
> The nearness of a notable Lover and Liberator.

The NAMER (Eph. 3:14-16)
> The foresight and foreknowledge of the Faithful Witness.

The NEW NAME (Rev. 3:12)
> The dignity of stately distinction superseded.

The NAZARITE (Num. 6:2-3)
> The one Character wholly free from the smear and fear of sin.

The NOURISHER (Isa. 1:2; Ruth 4:14-15)
> The supreme Source and Supplier of spiritual sustenance.

The NEWSBRINGER (Nah. 1:15; Matt. 11:5-6)
> The Hope of the downcast and Heralder of dawn.

The NUMBERER (Ps. 147:4-5; Matt. 10:30)
> The Lord conjoins infinite knowledge with intimate kindness.

The NOBLEMAN (Luke 19:9-13)
> The desirable Deliverer and His divine dignity.

The NOBLE NEGOTIATOR (Jer. 30:21; Heb. 13:20)
> The repletely righteous One who reconciles and represents.

The NEIGHBOR (Zech. 13:7; Luke 10:29-37)
> The Firstborn in fidelity, and foremost in friendliness.

The NAZARENE (Matt. 2:23)
    The life free from all artful and artificial adornments.

A NAME ABOVE EVERY NAME

The values of His victory are more virtuous
The comforts of His compassion are more copious
The legacies of His love are more lustrous
The gifts of His grace are more generous
The favors of His friendship are more famous
The pledges of His promise are more precious
The works of His wisdom are more wondrous

THAT AT THE NAME OF JESUS
EVERY KNEE SHOULD BOW

Oh, precious name! that perfects peace,
The hopeful pledge of full release;
That lifts us out of loss and pain,
To share Thine own eternal gain.

Oh, gracious name! love's purest ray,
That sheds glad joy through endless day,
Thy radiant light assures our right,
With title clear to glory bright.

Oh, generous name! that towers above,
Excelling all in perfect love,
To fill the heart and thrill the soul,
Proclaiming peace from pole to pole.

Oh, spacious name! that spans the years,
Dispelling grief and quelling fears;
Love's greatest good, God's Fatherhood,
Who sent the Son in Saviourhood.

Oh, wondrous name; that doth prepare,
True access to the throne in prayer,
That bids us take the children's place,
To meet the Father face to face.

Oh, glorious name! that heartens hope,
That points beyond time's utmost scope;
A mine of truth, eternal health,
The treasured source of lasting wealth.

Oh, lustrous name! so full of grace,
So fathomless we fain would trace,
Thy boundless love without a shore,
And revel in Thee evermore.

C. J. R.

I am Alpha and Omega (Rev. 22:13).

In the person of Christ we meet a whole world of wealth, a vast territory of treasure, a spacious ocean of fullness, a veritable vault of virtue, a resourceful reservoir of righteousness, and a capacious continent of comeliness. In the New Testament, believers are exhorted to grow in grace and in the knowledge of the Lord Jesus Christ, and this may best be achieved by diligently studying the many variegated splendors of His transcendent Name. As we advance in such a course of investigation, an ever-expanding enlightenment, together with an ever-widening discernment of His matchless glories opens before the mind. We shall never rightly comprehend the content of the Bible until we concentrate our attention on the Son of God, who is the sole center of all the divine purposes of grace and glory. The whole edifice of revealed truth is fashioned and furnished with one predominant objective, namely, graphically to portray the reality, dignity, mystery, and finality of the Person of Christ. The entire volume of Scripture directs our minds and hearts to one lonely form, lordly in honor, lowly in heart, and lovely in humility. This is He who not only designs but also determines and directs all things according to the counsel of His own immutable will. He Himself constitutes in His manifold character, the Door of destiny, the Key of knowledge, the Hinge of history, the Fount of faith, the Well of wisdom, the Root of royalty, the Tree of truth, the Branch of blessing, the Fulcrum of fullness, the Heritage of hope, and the Sum Total of sublimity. His voluminous name is vibrant with virtuous fame, constant with vigorous fidelity, and militant with victorious fortitude.

The ideal function of a name is to convey an accurate and concise description of the person or place to which the designation is appended. In relation to deity, this is always so and the meaning of the name is not only abidingly true of the character and disposition behind it, but also accurately sets forth the significance of the function and vocation that is being discharged. Every essential feature or inherent attribute of Christ that goes to comprise the totality of His status in Lordship, Headship, Heirship, and Kingship, together with every office He holds and vocation He fills, whether it be in love, life, or labor, we find expressed in a name or a title. Every qualification of honor and every quality of heart has its special designation to certify His capability. Our blessed Lord in every sphere in which we may view Him, whether in the capacity of the celestial or terrestrial, exercises a regency that is realistic, a ministry that is majestic, a sovereignty that is sympathetic, and an authority that is authentic. A beauty environs His dignified character and a ring of reality attends His delightful conduct. He is never taken by surprise, never startled with fear, and never hindered by inability.

The Apostle Peter gave utterance to a significant statement when he wrote the words, "Unto you therefore which believe He is the preciousness." Christ in His regal administration is forever righteous, and His righteousness is like the radiance of the sun whose light never develops or diminishes. In His judicial authority He is always just, and His justice is like the motion of the whirring wind which never tires or terminates. In His redemptive ministry He always recovers that which has been forfeited, and His redemption is alike in volume to the wide, wide ocean which never swells nor shrinks. In His faithful constancy He is wondrously balanced and His changeless faithfulness is like the stars which never vary or vanish.

Our blessed Lord, when He lifted His eyes to contemplate the glory of His coming Kingdom, was vividly conscious of its corruptless character, wherein myriads would revel in the liberty of life eternal, the society of love immortal, the stability of peace and the ecstasy of joys supernal. He was fully aware that of "the increase of His government and peace there shall be no end" (Isa. 9:7). The undisrupted oneness of a universal administration and the undisturbed harmony of a perfect unification of all things has been clearly revealed (Eph. 1:9,10).

Disagreement, disunion, and disintegration are to depart forever, and the everlasting kingdom of harmony, unison and unanimity is to be established evermore. In order to secure such a kingdom, Christ descended from the highest pinnacle of power to the lowest level of dishonor, rendered the fullest obedience in sacrificial service, defeated in spiritual conflict the strongest foe, finished the greatest work ever purposed, paid the largest liability ever incurred, ransomed the most extensive estate ever forfeited, and gained the greatest victory ever secured by overcoming death. All power to establish an everlasting and abiding kingdom is absolutely assured to the Conqueror who is the Ancient of Days. The enthronement of His excellency amid the spacious splendor of Heaven, and the magnificent majesty of His coronation at the right hand of the Most High justly warrant our expectation of a perfect and durable kingdom (Heb. 12:28).

Let us continue our course of procedure by selecting twelve of the names and titles by which Christ was known, commencing with the letter N.

THE NAME ABOVE EVERY NAME

Who, being in the form of God, thought not equality with God a thing to be held tenaciously, but made Himself of no reputation and took upon Him the form of a servant, and was made in the likeness of men: And being found in fashion as a man He humbled Himself and became obedient unto death even the death of the cross. Wherefore God also hath highly exalted Him and given Him a name which is above every name (Phil. 2:6-9 RV).

Four illuminating statements are made in the New Testament that throw a flood of light upon the inward nature of our Lord and Saviour. In these the heart of Christ is described clearly and concisely (Matt. 11:29). The will of Christ is declared briefly and beautifully (John 17:24). The mind of Christ is disclosed profoundly and perfectly (Phil. 2:5), and the love of Christ is displayed right royally and radiantly (1 John 3:16).

Our present title is taken from the context of the third of these four features and is found in conjunction with the disclosure of His mind.

Of all the lists of the famous of whom the world boasts, Christ is the sole dignitary who had a reputation, for He is the only one who ever appeared as a man among men unsubjected to death. There is no reputation in death.

> The world's a city with many a crooked street
> And in death's market place all men meet,
> If life were merchandise that men could buy,
> The rich alone would live and poor men die.

When the body of General Ulysses Grant, expresident of the United States, lay cold and silent, Stephen Merritt, the well-known undertaker of New York, was summoned to arrange for the burial. Upon entering the room he looked upon the form of one on whom the world's highest honors had been conferred by the greatest statesmen and national leaders of the universe. After locking both doors of entrance, he said in solitude, "Oh God, is this the end of human greatness?" Then kneeling reverently, he rededicated his life to Christian service, realizing, as he did so, that honor gained in such employ would outlive death and outlast the ages.

Our blessed Saviour, who was altogether immune from the power of death, made Himself of no reputation, and "became obedient unto death, even the death of the cross," and there is no manner of death more shameful and ignominious. Therefore God has highly exalted Him. That which He temporarily forfeited by submitting to death, He has gained eternally in a far greater degree of inexpressible honor.

If Christ were a mere man, the self-humiliation would have no meaning, for the renunciation of reputation was not possible for any ordinary human being to enact. All men had already forfeited reputation and were subjected to death, but Christ Himself stood alone, undeceived, undefeated, and undaunted. When the first Adam sought to exalt himself, he was humiliated, but the last Adam humbled himself and was exalted. Man, on account of his disobedience, was made subject to death, which meant the tragic loss of all reputation. On the other hand, Christ, on the basis of becoming obedient unto death, secured the stupendous triumph of resurrection and gained a glorious reputation for righteousness, which surmounts death and survives the ages, wherefore He has a Name which is above every Name. The Saviour has secured eternal advantages for man, as well as attracting everlasting adoration by virtue of His matchless victory over the devil and death.

In the light of comprehending the utmost values of the complete conquest, the eternal God anointed Him above His companions and accorded Him a Name above every name. The immortal distinction of such a stately designation and the infinite splendor of His unfading grandeur cause the eternal dominions of the Son of man to reverberate with anthems of adoring gratitude from myriads of the redeemed.

Here we face afresh those abysmal depths of impenetrable mystery, in that the Prince of princes, the King of kings, the Lord of lords, and the God of gods, undertakes to make Himself of no reputation by submitting to the meanest method of death, that of being crucified on the cursed tree.

Lifted to the loftiest heights in the realms of light, He is now enthroned, holiest in humility and highest in honor. His very name is a synonym for salvation, sanctification, and sovereignty. By virtue of His coronation at the pinnacle of supreme power, true excellence is exalted exceedingly, pure magnificence is magnified munificently, and rare majesty is multiplied manifoldly. Scripture affirms that He ascended up far above all heavens, and He justly and worthily merits the all-glorious honors conferred. The accomplishments of His reconciliation are more auspicious, the plans of His purpose are more ponderous, and the blessings He bestows are more bounteous than those any other personality ever brought to mankind. But such achievements do not constitute the main reason why He is the object of admiring wonder and the subject of adoring praise.

The Lord Himself in His own perfect character transcends His noblest work and far exceeds the greatest deeds He ever wrought. "He ... loved us ... and hath given Himself for us" (Eph. 5:2). To this the apostle adds, "He ... loved me, and gave Himself for me" (Gal. 2:20).

Consider Him, contemplate Him, for space is too small a sphere to provide Him a dwelling place, nay, the Heaven of heavens cannot contain Him. Time is too short a span to prepare for Him a footstool. Height is too low an altitude to exalt His name and fame. Thunder is too faint in volume to voice His praise and perfection. The ocean is too circumscribed in expanse to bespeak His fullness and faithfulness. The wind is too frail in its force to foreshadow the power of His sovereignty and supremacy. The stars are too dim in their brightness to reflect the brilliance of His glory and majesty. Immensity is too meager in degree to depict His immutability and immortality. A glimpse of this Blessed One broadens the horizons of vision and begets bigger and better conceptions of spiritual beauties and celestial realities. The royalty of His all-superior, all-subduing love elevates His dignity higher than the highest. The regality of His all-sufficient, all-sovereign power exhibits His dominion as mightier than the mightiest. The regency of His all-pervading, all-prevailing might expresses His deity as being statelier than the stateliest.

The ten thousand love deeds of His virtuous life, the tremendous love deed of His vicarious death, and the transcendent title deeds of His victorious heirship, signed with the signature of utmost importance and topmost influence, warrant our admiring wonder and adoring worship. Behold, He is mighty and despiseth not any. Hath He not said, "As the Father hath loved Me, so have I loved you" (John 15:9)? This is mercy's master-piece. When we contemplate the unsullied purity of Christ's whole being, it is not difficult to believe that in the integrity of His faithfulness there is not a shadow of turning. He is so entirely reliable that in the fidelity of His loving-kindness there is not an atom of indifference or the slightest lack of sympathetic care for a single sheep of His flock. He is so perfectly dependable that in the competency of His almightiness there is no trace of inability to fully accomplish His eternal purpose of gathering together all things in one, both which are in Heaven and which are in earth. The clarion note of the apocalypse heralds a new order, unique and universal, with a single society welded together in a wealthy display of worship, presented by one united voice unto Him who is worthy to receive power, and riches, and wisdom, and strength, and honor, and glory, and blessing (Rev. 5:13; 7:12).

Who, other than Christ, could produce from the diversities and disharmonies of mankind, a unified control and a united voice from every tribe and tongue and people and nation? The fulfillment of such an ideal, with equality of nature as one of its essential features, and with every expression of rapturous enjoy-ment in exercise, will be established eternally by the determi-nate counsel of the great Conqueror. The scene portraying these things is indescribably impressive, for every bond of affinity, every motive of sympathy, every custom of country and every trend of nationality is merged into perfect harmony, and the actor who achieves it does so on the basic fact of reconciliation, and is therefore deserving of a Name that is above every name. Where else may we turn in the hope of securing permanent agreement and perfect harmony between nation, race, creed, and class? If we consider Jew and Arab, black and white, rich and poor, cultured and ignorant, English and Irish, French and German, Italian and Austrian, Chinese and Japanese, Buddist and Brahman, we know of One alone who can banish all such distinctions and build a united sodality, a brotherhood founded on righteousness, fashioned in peaceableness, and favored with loving-kindness forever.

THE NEAR OF KIN

The man is near of kin (Ruth 2:20).
The king is near of kin to us (2 Sam. 19:42).
His kin, that is near unto him (Lev. 21:2).
His kinsman that is next (Num. 27:11).

The three words "next," "nigh," and "near," are used in Scripture of this reassuring relationship. The kin that was near had special functions to fulfill on behalf of those who needed help, wherever this familiar family tie existed. In all cases where possessions and privileges had been lost through adversity or forfeited because of poverty, the kinsfolk were required to inter-vene (Lev. 25:25). Job bemoaned the fact that they from whom he had a right to expect sympathy and support had deserted him. Said he, "My kinsfolk have failed, and my familiar friends have forgotten me" (Job 19:14). David likewise encountered a similar distress while reigning over Israel. Here are his ex-pressive words: "My lovers and my friends stand aloof from my sore; and my kinsmen stand afar off" (Ps. 38:11).

The pathetic plight of these men is keenly felt because they had a right to expect expressions of mutual aid, but failed to find such. However, the condition of mankind was far more tragic, because the forfeiture of all claim on life and liberty had led to a desperate state of affairs. Man looked longingly for someone to take pity on his plight, but among the ranks of humankind there was none in a position to help (Isa. 63:5).

When Ruth, the Moabitess, had been plunged into the sorrow of widowhood and poverty, the women of Bethlehem congratu-lated her mother-in-law by saying, "Blessed be the Lord, which hath not left thee this day without a kinsman" (Ruth 4:14). No stranger could intermeddle in these matters. The one indispens-able condition had been settled by divine decree, so that only one who was near of kin could intervene. The antitype of all this constitutes the sum and substance of the age-old, worldwide gospel story.

Man had become a slave to sin and Satan, and was made subject to death. Or as the Apostle Paul declares, "sold under sin" (Rom. 7:14). Therefore Christ was born into this world as Son of man to identify Himself with those ensnared by sin and enslaved by Satan. Being found in fashion as a man, He qualified by becoming man, to redeem humanity. He took upon Him the seed of Abraham, and qualified Himself as a Hebrew to redeem Hebrews. He was made like to His brethren the Jews and was thereby qualified as the firstborn to redeem His brethren.

Christ ratified and perfectly fulfilled all that the Hebrew law required so that He might stand in right relationship, legitimately and legally qualified to ransom the estate from the hand of Satan, the usurper, and redeem man from the thralldom of sin, and emancipate him from the power of death.

The character of this Redeemer together with some of the details of His great and gracious work are graphically depicted by the prophet Isaiah. He tells of Christ as a light to the nations and salvation to the ends of the earth, and goes on to declare, "Thus saith the Lord, In an acceptable time have I heard thee, and in a day of salvation have I helped thee: and I will preserve thee, and give thee for a covenant of the people, to establish the earth, to cause to inherit the desolate heritages; That thou mayest say to the prisoners, Go forth" (Isa. 49:8-9). The chapter ends by stating, "all flesh shall know that I the Lord am thy Saviour and thy Redeemer, the mighty One of Jacob" (verse 26).

Blessed be the Lord who has not left us without a near of kin, One who never deserts, who never disappoints, and who never denies those in distress a hearing ear or a helping hand. "The LORD is nigh unto all them that call upon Him, to all that call upon Him in truth" (Ps. 145:18). "The LORD is nigh unto them that are of a broken heart; and saveth such as be of a contrite spirit" (Ps. 34:18). Such assurances are prolific in the Word of God. "He is near that justifieth me" (Isa. 50:8). "My righteousness is near" (Isa. 51:5). "Call ye upon Him while He is near" (Isa. 55:6). How wonderful that we who were once far off have been made nigh through our near of kin, the Son of man!

In the remarkable chapter that speaks of bringing back the king of Israel to Jerusalem after a season of exile, the men of Israel asked David why they had not been consulted in the matter. In answering this query the men of Judah said emphatically, "Because the king is near of kin to us" (2 Sam. 19:42). What a thrilling statement this is when it is applied to the people of God. When the Son of God appeared in human form as Son of man, He came to ransom us from bondage and make us partakers of the divine nature. Let us remember that the One who wrought this wonderful work is none other than the King of kings. Therefore this King is near of kin to us. What amazing news this becomes to prisoners who are in a cruel bondage. No wonder they are spoken of as prisoners of hope (Zech. 9:11-12). The verse preceding is precious to the soul: "He shall speak peace to the nations and His dominion shall be from sea even to sea, and from the river to the ends of the earth. As for thee also by the blood of thy covenant I have sent forth thy prisoners out of the pit where is no water" (Zech. 9:10-11). This at first seems a strange epitaph — prisoners of hope. Notice what precedes: "Behold, thy King cometh unto thee: He is just, and having salvation" (Verse 9).

In Field Castle on the Isle of Wight there is an old solidly built prison. Above the facade of the large dungeon which faces the sea is the deeply-cut inscription, "Hope Cell." This seems a strange anomaly, but how true it really was. Political prisoners were sent to this prison by the ruling king whose power they had challenged or had sought to usurp. Each one incarcerated was compelled to remain there during the life of the reigning monarch. When the king died, however, the prisoners were loosed, hence they always lived in the hope that the king would die during their lifetime that they might be released from prison and have freedom.

The gospel narrative tells how the King of kings came to this earth in manifestation, and that He died in order to deliver us from him who had the power of death, that is the devil (Heb. 2:15).

My chains are snapped, the bonds of sin are broken and I am free,
  Oh, let the triumphs of His grace be spoken, who died for me.

THE NAMER

For this cause I bow my knees unto the Father of our Lord Jesus Christ, of whom the whole family in heaven and earth is named, That He would grant you, according to the riches of His glory, to be strengthened with might by His Spirit (Eph. 3:14-16).

At this juncture we are introduced to a complete system of seven notable contrasts which are made between the first man Adam, the federal head of the natural race, and the second Man, the last Adam, which is Christ, who is the federal head of the spiritual race. In connection with these two conspicuous personalities we become acquainted with two familiar gardens, the Garden of Eden and the Garden of Gethsemane; and two formidable acts, one of disobedience and one of obedience; and two far-reaching issues, "many were made sinners" and "many were made righteous."

However, we are at present interested in the two famous functions that were discharged by these two federal heads, that is, the bestowing and recording of names. The first Adam was the original namer of all the creatures round about him, for it is written, "And out of the ground the Lord God formed every beast of the field, and every fowl of the air; and brought them unto Adam to see what he would call them: and whatsoever Adam called every living creature, that was the name thereof. And Adam gave names to all cattle, and to the fowl of the air, and to every beast of the field" (Gen. 2:19-20).

Man, being a direct creation of God, had an intuitive knowledge that was manifold and mature. The fact of alphabet, language, wisdom, and knowledge existed before man was created, for the Scriptures supply us with a record of what God said and what He did prior to the creation of man. These are matters outside the range of human investigation, and can only be known by means of revelation. The marvelous characteristics associated with this function of naming everything on the part of the first Adam, who had no lexicon or encyclopedia, furnishes a suggestive finger-post, which directs us to the action of the last Adam, the Lord from Heaven, by whom every family in Heaven and earth is named. Naming was one of the initial things associated with this physical creation, and it is likewise one of the essential things relative to the spiritual family of the household of God. The great Shepherd-Creator who calls all the stars by name in the greatness of His might as declared in Isaiah 40, is depicted as the same Creator-Shepherd who calls His own sheep by name in the graciousness of His majesty (John 10:3). This is but another of the numerous portrayals of the infinite intelligence that characterizes our wondrous Shepherd-Saviour in the capacity of His deity.

Similar features to these of our Lord's Godhead are again combined in the reassuring proclamation of the prophet, "thus saith the Lord that created thee, O Jacob, and He that formed thee, O Israel, Fear not: for I have redeemed thee, I have called thee by thy name; thou art Mine" (Isa. 43:1). Indeed, the whole house of Israel was named by this Namer. When the twelve tribes were named, the Lord had in mind His ultimate purpose and by virtue of His foreknowledge and foresight He determined for them names that had meanings which were suitable to signify the characteristics and qualifications for entrance into the city of God. He foreknew that their twelve names were destined to be inscribed on the twelve gates which were each likened to one special pearl (Rev. 21:12).

Only an omniscient mind could have designed such a purpose and prepared its details thousands of years before the permanent features of that perfected society were to be made manifest. The Lord has adopted various channels to set before our minds the all-inclusive comprehension which characterizes His foreknowledge. One of those is the making known beforehand the names by which certain individuals would be known. The Scriptures record seven instances of this, in which the designa- tions of persons as yet unborn were revealed months, years, and centuries before they appeared in this world. King Cyrus is an example and is called by name over two centuries before his birth (Isa. 45:1-4). "Known unto God are all His works from the beginning of the world" (Acts 15:18).

We have to do with One whose wisdom is infinite, whose knowledge is perfect, whose understanding is complete and whose awareness of past, present, and future is absolute. Verily, He is fully aware of every name of everyone everywhere, for all things are naked and open unto the eyes of Him with whom we have to do (Heb. 4:12-13). Are we daily conscious that He knows and loves and cares? For He stands hard by and is not far from every one of us. "For in Him we live, and move, and have our being; as certain also of your own poets have said, For we are also His offspring" (Acts 17:28).

The gospel records disclose that Christ never needed to be introduced to anyone, for there was no one anywhere whom He did not know. When Philip was approaching with his friend, Christ said of Nathaniel, "Behold an Israelite indeed, in whom is no guile!" Startled by the accuracy of the description, Nathan- iel inquired, "Whence knowest thou me?"

He received the reply, "Before that Philip called thee, when thou wast under the fig tree, I saw thee." On another occasion, when Andrew sought out his brother Simon, and was approach- ing the Master, He looked up and said "Thou art Simon, son of John, thou shalt be called Cephas, rock." John is careful to tell us that Christ did not need anyone to acquaint Him concerning anyone else, for He knew all men (John 2:24). At the time His disciples returned from their first campaign they rehearsed to their Lord what had been accomplished, and were specially glad over the fact that evil spirits had been subject to their power.

The Lord immediately turned their attention to a more pro- found cause for joy. Said He, "rejoice not, that the spirits are subject unto you; but rather rejoice because your names are written in heaven" (Luke 10:17-20). No one ever possessed this knowledge save He who came down from Heaven. Were not the members of His mystical body written in the Book of Life, when as yet there were none of them? (Ps. 139:16) The Apostle Paul, when speaking of his co-workers who labored with him in the gospel, said with confidence, "whose names are in the book of life" (Phil. 4:3). That our Lord knows the names of all His redeemed people from the beginning, for He named them, is the essence of truth's verity, the voice of wisdom's veracity, the soul of shepherd-sympathy and the sweetness of His superior sovereignty.

> Forget thee I will not, I cannot. Thy name,
> Engraved on My heart doth forever remain.
> The palms of my hands while I look on I see,
> The wounds I received when suffering for thee.

THE NEW NAME

Him that overcometh will I make a pillar in the temple of My God, and he shall go no more out: and I will write upon him the name of My God, and the name of the city of My God . . . new Jerusalem . . . and My new name (Rev. 3:12).

In the realm of nomenclature, which means a system of names, no record is more fascinating to investigate than the book of the Revelation of Jesus Christ. Our attention is arrested to find that the One who has previously been declared and described by the greatest catalog of distinctive designations of any personality known, herein makes reference to His New Name.

We may naturally conclude, after tabulating over six hundred of the Saviour's names and titles of dignity and divinity that appear in the previous books of the Bible, that it would be exceedingly difficult to declare any fresh phase of His fame by using a new name. But that difficulty can never arise in the case of the Christ of God. Herein we discover titles more wondrous in their range of meaning and more ponderous in their wealth of renown than any that have gone before. These are supplied for the purpose of more fully disclosing the true character of Christ to His people so that we may the more completely identify the real nature of His absolute deity. Furthermore, the unveiling displays with greater vividness the vastness of the consequences of the covenant He confirmed during the manifestation, so that the final issues might be more clearly interpreted.

The word *new* is used seven times in the book of the Revelation, and is attached variously, including a new name, a new Jerusalem, a new song, a new happiness, a new Heaven, a new earth, and the making of all things new. If we are to appreciate the significance of the new name, we need to examine what is involved. In order to do so it is necessary to survey the four outstanding features of consummation in the four great divisions of the book. We must be prepared to ascend the loftiest mountain of aspiration to view the One who overcame and sat down with His Father upon His throne, amid the greatest display of celestial splendor ever imagined (Rev. 3:21).

We should definitely resolve to transverse the broadest domains of possession in a fadeless inheritance until we visualize the Chief Shepherd leading by fountains of living water and wiping away all tears in the entrancing beauty of Beulah Land (Rev. 7:14, 17). We should aspire to survey the immeasurable powers of dominion swayed by the scepter of His enduring authority, which He exercises as Priest-King without any trace of misuse or abuse of office, when the world kingdom becomes His age-abiding kingdom (Rev. 11:15).

Then again we are required to scan the magnitude and magnificence of an infinite justice, flawless in finding verdicts and faultless in issuing sentences, which qualifies Him to quell all evil, in order to make all things new and establish the perfect society of the city of God (Rev. 20-21).

In the light of such astounding achievements, what in the way of a new name could possibly be chosen that would suitably describe so competent a Champion, who overcomes all opposition to the divine will and is coronated at the right hand of the Majesty in the heavens? What in the whole wide world could be selected as a designation that would adequately befit so complete a Custodian, who prevails over the usurper and takes the title deeds to the entire universe, for the purpose of administering the divine will on earth as in Heaven? What selection from the myriads of existing names would be appropriate for so celebrated a Conqueror, who overthrows all opposition and secures in His triumphant campaign the final defeat of the devil, the downfall of antichristian agitators, the doom of Babylon, the displacement of evil, and the destruction of death, and who fully establishes the will of God? Where may we obtain from the annals of history an appropriate title for so capable a consummator, who terminates thorns, trials, tears, and tombs, who transcends the sun in its glory, and transmutes the souls of men into the divine image, to live and love in eternal harmony and holiness with the will of God? The records of all the registry offices of the nations may be searched, the renowned philosophers may be called together to consider and consult with one another, but all in vain. No one is capable of proposing or propounding suitable names for a celebrity of such caliber.

We are confined to a single source for the information we seek and if we are ever to know, we must allow the Lord of Glory to speak for Himself. This Beloved Christ of God, by virtue of the variety of His titles already disclosed, also in view of the universality of His claims already verified, and in the light of the authority of His powers already demonstrated, stands unprecedented in wisdom, unparalleled in knowledge, and unsurpassed in understanding.

The first sunburst which is so radiant with new luster emanated from the One "who is the faithful witness, and the first begotten of the dead, and the prince of the kings of earth" (Rev. 1:5). This triple title expresses the integrity of His ministry which is winsome, the victory of His mastery over death which is welcome, and the authority of His majesty above all royalties of renown which is wonderful and widespread.

The next triune title characterized by newness expands the range of Christ's regality to a length, breadth, and height wholly undefinable. In this case His words are exquisite in their descriptive dignity, and most excellent in divine distinction. "I am the Alpha and Omega, the beginning and the ending, saith the Lord, which is, and which was, and which is to come, the Almighty" (Rev. 1:8).

In this new Name of claim the Lord declares Himself to be the Repository and Reservoir of all wisdom and knowledge, the Originator and Overseer of all official rank and power, and the almighty Administrator who resides and abides in supreme control everywhere eternally. John was in banishment on Patmos because of his testimony to his beloved Lord, and links himself with all bond servants who suffer tribulation in the interests of the kingdom. Wherefore to all warriors in conflict with evil, these exceptional titles have proved to be springs of refreshment and reservoirs of reinvigoration in trial from age to age. Christ Himself overcame and is set down with His Father on His throne, because of which He encourages His servants to endure and likewise overcome.

Let us select another of these threefold titles which was revealed for the purpose of arresting declension in a decadent church. "These things saith the Amen, the faithful and true witness, the beginning of the creation of God" (Rev. 3:14).

In the place of the faint glimmers of His greatness as seen in the Gospel records, we are now introduced to the glowing outbursts of His transcendent glories. The highest honor ever conferred is centered in this most coveted of titles, the Amen. Christ is the only One qualified to receive such a significant designation, because He confirmed and carried out every command of God. He is therefore the personification of perfect obedience in all things, the everliving certitude of the everlasting Word. We may speak of this as one of the newest and most notable of His never-fading names. Let us sum up this triple title by saying, He is unfaltering in His complete conformity to the Word of God, the Observer of every ordinance, the Amen, to verify every syllable of truth. He is unfailing in His consistent witness to the will of God, the Orator of the eternal oracles, the faithful and true Witness. He is unfeigning in His complacent claim to the work of God, the Originator of the existing order, the Beginning of the creation of God. These towering features bespeak His omnipresence, omniscience, and omnipotence which are so frequently found in combination. We must needs pass by the Lion of the tribe of Judah and the Word of God, although of the latter it is stated that He had on His head many diadems and He had a name written that no one knew but He Himself . . . and His name is called "The Word of God" (Rev. 19:11-13).

Let us conclude with mentioning the last triple title the Lord proclaimed to John. "I am the root and the offspring of David and the bright, the morning star" (Rev. 22:16 RV). No one, other than Christ Himself, used language to express names and titles as He did. His statements are not only unique, they are unsurpassed in their range of dimension, realm of dominion, and rank of distinction. In this case He harnesses the historic, prophetic, and symbolic features and makes them contribute yet another chaplet to His worthy brow. A root, an offshoot, and a bright star are blended to express characteristics that span the entire range from zero to zenith, and from start to finish in history, prophecy, and reality. The lowly life of His earthly manifestation on the one side is linked with His lofty lineage and heavenly ministration on the other. The combination of metaphors from the humblest figure of a root to the highest feature of a star traverses the whole continent of influence from that which is silent and concealed to that which scintillates most conspicuously everywhere.

We should remember the Friend of sinners is also the fullness of Godhead and First-born of all creation. The Shepherd of the sheep is the same who sustains the stars. He commences His great masterpiece of creation and the creature silently as the Root, and in His continuity of the great work of construction He is manifest as the Offshoot of David, at the center of His Church, standing in the midst of the great congregation (Ps. 22:22). Ultimately He is the Circumference, and crowns His work with completion at His glorious coming, for He shall arise as the Morning Star to usher in eternal day. Christ is the unseen source from whence David sprang, the Root of all royalty, of which David was the consummate flower of kinghood in Israel. For it is written, "By me kings reign, and princes decree justice" (Prov. 8:15).

This final of all revealed titles warrants our saying that it suggests the invisibility of an undisclosed prescience of One who in His precedence is the Sustainer of all. Secondly, it signifies the intimacy of His undisguised personality who in His permanence is the Saviour of all men. Thirdly, it stipulates the infinity of His underived preeminence, who in His providence is the Supervisor of all peoples eternally. We say without hesitancy that in this closing book of the Bible there is a peerless, matchless, fadeless newness about the precious and priceless name of our beloved and blessed Lord Jesus. The crowning prevalence of His infinite merit, by virtue of which He redeems millions of souls, the copious plenitude of His indispensable mercy in reconciling myriads to God by His death and the covenant permanence of His immortal majesty in His ruling innumerable multitudes in perfect peace forever, worthily warrants and justly claims this multiform New Name.

THE NAZARITE

When either man or woman shall separate to vow a vow of a Nazarite, to separate unto the Lord: He shall separate from wine and strong drink . . . neither shall he drink any liquor of grapes, nor eat moist grapes, or dried (Num. 6:2-3).

When we attempt to describe the virtues and victories of Christ in His many-sided character, we cannot touch the fringe of His splendor as a Kinsman-Redeemer, nor even reach the border of His grandeur as a kingly Reconciler, for in the accomplishment of such ministries He ascended to the highest pinnacle of renown, not only in this world, but in that which is to come. The mighty ranks Christ holds in every sphere of divine service, the many offices He fills, the masterly powers He sways, and the manifold titles He bears, contribute to the visible display of the inherent glory of His intrinsic character.

He solemnly averred to John at Jordan, "suffer it to be so now, for thus it becomes Us to fulfill all righteousness." He had come in an exemplary capacity, to carry out entirely and effectively the injunctions and functions which were enjoined in the Scripture of truth. During the manifestation He completely discharged all the obligations of the Firstborn, faithfully fulfilled the requirements of the Forerunner, and sedulously complied in meeting all demands as the Firstfruits.

As the Son of Man, He wholly conformed in performing the vow of the Nazarite, which required a fourfold submission. Such things as indulgences, intimacies, individualities, and influences that were common factors in the routine of most lives, were not to be allowed to constrain or control the soul that was separated unto the Lord. Both John and Jesus, like Samson and Samuel, were Nazarites from birth.

The specified indulgences were signified in the figures of wine and liquors, together with partaking of the grape which was not to be used, and in regard to the latter it was to be excluded from the husk to the kernel, moist or dried.

The social intimacies were suggested in the entire range of relationships and the Nazarite was required to withdraw from all familiar ties, ranging from wife to kinsfolk. All such aspects of association were to be relinquished during the period of the vow. The special individualities or idiosyncrasies were indicated by matters connected with one's own personal life and concerned the whole man, from his will to determine, on to his kingship in dominion over creation. No room of any kind was to be made for self-assertiveness or self-government. The hair of the head was to be allowed to grow long, which suggested subjection to divine authority at all times, in all things.

The surrounding influences were implied in property possessed and in wealth of resource, which might be of avail in furnishing luxuries, so that from kindly ministries of such sort a person would be enabled to live independently and partake of whatsoever food was desired. Therefore anyone undertaking the vow must needs abandon any accumulated treasure or riches.

If we carefully consider the ministry of Christ depicted in the four gospel records, and compare His methods of life and the statements He made on different occasions, in the light of the fourfold obligation of this vow, we shall be absolutely amazed at the measure in which He carried out every requirement perfectly. Never once did He allow the nominal things of every-day life to divert His attention from supreme matters. When His disciples appeared with food which they had procured in Samaria and sought to induce Him to eat while He was speaking to an interested soul, He answered, "I have meat to eat that ye know not of," and again, "My meat is to do the will of Him that sent me and to finish His work."

On no occasion did He permit natural affection to deflect His devotion from His one great aim, nay, not even the request of His mother derived any attention (from Him) whatsoever.

Not one single instance occurred in which national ideas determined His activities or aspirations, so that He was able to say when speaking of the Father, "I do always those things that please Him" and again, "I came not to do Mine own will, but the will of Him that sent Me." "When Jesus therefore perceived that they would come and take Him by force, to make Him a king, He departed again into a mountain Himself alone" (John 6:15). Not the slightest sign of a case appears in which He permitted natural advantages to deter Him from wholehearted dependence on the Father for strength, supply, and security. He was resolute in His reliance, always and altogether. Although He made bread for the needs of others, He refused to make any for His personal needs, even when challenged by the devil to do so in the wilderness.

We may notice from the chapter which supplies our title that the path of the true Nazarite was marked by four outstanding characteristics. These comprised the evidences of separation, the expressions of dedication, the experience of humiliation, and the enduring benediction of the triune God. All four of these were most obviously exemplified in the life of the Son of man.

The minute instructions that were given in connection with the Nazarite vow reflect the highest refinement of divine wisdom. Not even the slightest detail of the Law was left to human intelligence for decision, no more than a single loop or tache in the tabernacle pattern was the product of man's mind.

The Lord made it quite clear that He required a special physical fitness of nature, a moral suitability of character combined with spiritual virtues of heart and mind as qualifications on the part of those that sought to serve Him.

Our beloved Saviour demonstrated that He was perfectly adapted to render the self-denying, self-sacrificing service demanded for the purpose of securing salvation for mankind. He knew full well all the violations of virtue that had transpired, and set Himself with invincible resolve to satisfy the claims of divine justice and become the Saviour of all who obey Him (Heb. 5:9).

Anyone who aspires to become a surgeon must acquaint himself with the anatomy of the human body ere he can be skillful in adjusting a broken limb. Said a lady at a clinic, "I desire Dr. So-and-So to attend to me, for I know him to be fully conversant with my complaint." Christ fully understands the sinfulness of sin, the severity of divine justice against it, and the remedial measures necessary for redemption. When we turn to observe our Saviour's full obedience to the law of the Nazarite, and how thoroughly His stainless life was fortified against the entanglements, enticements, excitements, and entertainments that would mar and endanger His suitability as a perfect sacrifice, we marvel at the weight of merit manifest in the presenting of Himself without spot to God. Christ most certainly demonstrated His adaptability to become a Deliverer from the fourfold menace brought about because of the degeneracy of human nature, the dominion of sin, the dominance of the devil, and the doom of death. The Levitical law was explicit and declared concerning the sacrificial offering presented, "It shall be perfect to be accepted for thee" (Lev. 22:21). The entire life of Christ diffused the sunshine of Heaven's perfect love, and His Cross demonstrated forever His perfect obedience to the Father's will.

THE NOURISHER

Hear, O heavens and give ear, O earth; for the Lord hath spoken, I have nourished and brought up children, and they have rebelled against Me (Isa. 1:2).

Blessed be the Lord, which hath not left thee this day without a kinsman, that his name may be famous in Israel. And he shall be unto thee a restorer of thy life, and a nourisher of thine old age (Ruth 4:14-15).

One of the first instructions the Creator gave after He had made man concerned the sustenance that was necessary for his maintenance. When addressing the creature God said, "Of every tree of the garden thou mayest freely eat"; then He added a single restriction as a mark of superior authority. Centuries later Noah received more detailed instruction, while Moses, the legislator, had committed to him a complete system of laws for the nourishment of the nation of Israel. Verily, the presence, power, and provision of God in their relation to the revelation of His eternal purpose permeate the whole of Scripture.

The regulations for the support of the physical nature foreshadowed the deeper need of provision being made for the development of moral stamina and spiritual strength. That is why feeding upon the manna, roast lamb, firstfruits, and corn signified a more abundant provision on a higher plane, ultimately to be disclosed in the bread of God and the water of life, so wonderfully assured in Christ Jesus the Lord.

From the light of His lovely countenance and friendly fellowship, the spiritual capacities are all furnished with the precious products which are later pictured as procurable from the Tree of Life, standing in the midst of the paradise of God. The reason that righteousness, peace, and joy flourish forever is because all such commodities are maintained through the riches in glory by Christ Jesus, who is all the Fullness of God. Prayer, praise, and perfectness are likewise lavishly sustained by His replete resource, for His is the reservoir of reserve supplies. Unless He constantly nourished spiritual capacities and faculties, no soul could continually flourish in moral excellence and immortal beauty.

One of the most eminent and notable portrayals of Christ to be found in the whole of Scripture is centered in the life and ministry of Joseph. This most honored son of Jacob rose to the highest rank of administration in Egypt and became the nourisher and sustainer of the civilized world. But his famous work was not confined to the large communities. He likewise had respect for his own people's needs and high regard for his aging father's requirements.

"And Joseph nourished his father, and his brethren, and all his father's household, with bread, according to their families" (Gen. 47:12). After Jacob's decease, anxiety arose in the minds of his sons as to whether Joseph would retaliate and inflict some injury on them, because of what they had done to him in earlier life, but his answer is most reassuring, "And Joseph said unto them. . . . Now therefore fear ye not: I will nourish you, and your little ones. And he comforted them, and spake kindly unto them" (Gen. 50: 19, 21). He was able to say unto his brethren, "Ye thought evil against me, but God meant it unto good." The divine providence is so unmistakably evident in making adequate provision over against the day of emergency that we are well within the bounds of relevancy in referring this title of Nourisher to our blessed Saviour.

Nehemiah knew in his household at Jerusalem what it meant to nourish at his own table over one hundred and fifty workers daily, for over two months. This he did at his own expense (Neh. 5;17). The conditions that existed caused him to look back and reflect on the history of the nation and recount somewhat of the lavish provision God had made for them. "Thou gavest them bread from heaven for their hunger, and broughtest forth water for them out of the rock. . . . Yea, forty years didst Thou sustain [same word as nourish] them in the wilderness, so that they lacked nothing" (Neh. 9:15, 21).

Because the Lord is characterized by infinite gladness, He is capable of experiencing most intense grief, and therefore calls upon Heaven and humanity to give heed to the nature of Israel's offense. He affirms, "I have nourished and brought up children, and they have rebelled against Me" (Isa. 1:2). The Lord lamented because as the great and generous Nourisher He was ignored, and as the lavish Provider and Preserver He was spurned by His people. All material mercies for physical well-being besides all spiritual blessings for moral welfare, are furnished by His generous hand. A figure of this liberality is beautifully expressed by the women of Bethlehem saying to Naomi, "Blessed be the Lord, which hath not left thee this day without a kinsman, that his name may be famous in Israel. And he shall be unto thee a restorer of thy life, and a nourisher of thine old age" (Ruth 4:14-15).

— The nearer the Lord's people live to this bountiful Supplier, the happier, healthier, and heartier they become. Let us not grieve the delicate sensitiveness of His infinite heart by base indifference and baneful ingratitude. The weighty supplies furnished to the Egyptians was soon forgotten; there arose a Pharaoh that knew not Joseph, but how much more lavish Jesus was by virtue of His superior power. His kindness in feeding multitudes eclipsed all former expressions of bounty, the occasions of which served as convincing illustrations of His limitless resources of spiritual nourishment for sustaining the whole household of faith. What greater figure of this abounding and abiding sufficiency could be conceived than that of the Tree of Life in the midst of the paradise of God, yielding twelve manners of fruits every month, as a perpetual source of sustenance for maintaining unabatedly the innumerable hosts of the redeemed.

Christ is the true substance that supersedes all shadows. From Him emanates the meat which endureth unto everlasting life.

He stated the matter definitely by saying, "He that eateth of Me shall never hunger." The remarkable resources of this great Nourisher are not external. The woman of Samaria was startled when Christ told her of the well of life. "Why," she said, "the well is deep and Thou hast nothing to draw with, whence then hast Thou this living water?" He informed her that spiritual supplies were invisible to physical sight. He Himself is the essential sap of sustenance, the fountain of fullness, the reservoir of resource, and the storehouse of sufficiency. No external factors are capable of furnishing the soul with nutriment for the moral and spiritual nature. The Son of man is the sole source of supply. Where else may we turn and secure a portion of meat that in due season will nourish and build up in us a constitution of righteousness, goodness, loving-kindness, and holiness? Such realities and spiritual specialties are not derived at all from any human sources. Let us recall Oliver Cromwell's prayer for the people of England: "Lord, teach them to depend less upon Thine instruments and more upon Thyself."

"Thy words were found, and I did eat them; and Thy word was unto me the joy and rejoicing of mine heart" (Jer. 15:16). How tragic when men seek to tamper with Scripture, and tincture the infallible revelation of truth with human thoughts and reasonings! Let us keep hard by the deep well of the Saviour's sufficiency, lest we become weakly in well-being and weary in well-doing. This sympathetic Shepherd of Israel, this attentive Angel of the covenant, this Leader and Legislator of Sinai, this Commander and Controller of the seasons, this notable Nourisher of the wilderness, has an exhaustless supply of spiritual sustenance, and so therefore, was entitled to reveal Himself to John on Patmos as the Tree of Life in the midst of the paradise of God, yielding supplies every month in a dozen varieties for the unvarying maintenance of the hosts of the redeemed in their twelvefold delights.

All the elements of grace and of growth are ministered by the Revealer and Mediator of God. The genuine guarantee of this is given in the greatest figures of resource ever revealed to mankind, which describe Christ as being "all the fullness of the Godhead bodily, The Alpha and Omega, the beginning and the end, the first and the last, He which is, which was, and which is to come, the Almighty."

THE NEWSBRINGER

Behold upon the mountains the feet of him that bringeth good tidings (Nah. 1:15).

The Spirit of the Lord is upon Me, because He hath anointed Me to preach the gospel to the poor . . . and He began to say unto them, This day is this Scripture fulfilled in your ears. And all bare Him witness, and wondered at the gracious words that proceeded out of His mouth (Luke 4:18, 21-22).

The poor have the gospel preached to them. And blessed is he, whosoever shall not be offended in Me (Matt. 11:5-6).

No one else ever brought to mankind such good news and glad tidings as Christ did. His loving words were heaven-hewn and royal; His gracious sayings throbbed with the pulsations of the Father's heart of infinite mercy: "never man spake like this man." The angelic messenger intimated the arrival of this greatest Newsbringer by saying; "Fear not: for, behold, I bring you good tidings of great joy, which shall be to all people. For unto you is born this day in the city of David, a Saviour, which is Christ the Lord" (Luke 2:10-11).

Then the heavenly host immediately corroborated the glorious purpose of the manifestation (verse 14). At the commencement of the Saviour's ministry He made use of words in a manner such as no predecessor had ever done, by taking the familiar term "Amen," which had always been used at the close of a statement, and repeating it twice at the beginning of His utterance. In our authorized version the expression is rendered, "Verily, verily," which is actually "Amen, amen." Why did He preface twenty-four of His declarations with these words? Most definitely to arrest attention and attract the notice of His hearers to the nature of the news He was bringing to mankind. What a startling report is voiced in this first use when He said "Amen, amen, I say unto you, hereafter ye shall see heaven open" (John 1:51). What! An open Heaven? No one ever brought such wonderful news as this to man, who had long been excluded from those celestial realms. When affirming to John later that He had the key of David, Christ claims to be "He that openeth and no man shutteth" (Rev. 3:7).

Little wonder that He taught His disciples, "No man cometh unto the Father but by Me." No news ever brought to mankind is more enlightening, exhilarating, and encouraging than to know that the barriers which hindered man from access to God, and denied him entrance to the portals of the eternal, have been removed, and that an open Heaven is before all. "Him that cometh to Me I will in no wise cast out." Wherefore He went on to say, "Amen, amen, I say unto you, He that believeth on Me hath everlasting life" (John 6:47). Then said Jesus unto them again, "Amen, amen, I say unto you . . . I am the door: by Me if any man enter in, he shall be saved" (John 10:7,9). No literature exists in the whole wide world outside of Bible phraseology containing language comparable to this.

The quotation we have chosen from the prophecy of Nahum depicts a terrific flood with its overwhelming force, destroying everything in its wake, save one great fortress of rock, which provides the only secure refuge from the weltering ruin. The Assyrian invasion was devastating the land. Protection or preservation from this most cruel of ancient powers seemed an impossibility. At the crucial moment, when the capital city of Jerusalem itself was threatened, the Lord sent the prophet from the surrounding hills with the good news of deliverance. His message has never lost its charm and comfort. "The Lord is good, a stronghold in the day of trouble; and He knoweth them that trust in Him" (Nah. 1:7). What wonderful news for those harassed with foreboding trouble! The good Lord Himself assures the distressed that He is on guard as a fortified castle to the beseiged, as a strong tower to the bewildered, and as an impregnable bastion to those bereft of help. How deeply interesting it is to notice that one of the seven features used to describe the furious holocaust of judgment about to strike, is indicated by the word "vengeance" (Nah. 1:2). Precisely the same setting characterizes the conditions attending the message of the prophet Isaiah, which Christ read in the synagogue at Nazareth. "And when He had opened the book, He found the place where it was written, The Spirit of the Lord is upon Me, because He hath anointed me to preach the gospel to the poor; He hath sent Me to heal the brokenhearted, to preach deliverance to the captives, and recovering of sight to the blind, to set at liberty them that are bruised, To preach the acceptable year of the Lord" (Luke 4:17-19). The next sentence in the prophecy declares, "and the day of vengeance of our God" (Isa. 61:2).

What a heartening testimony Christ bore, the day of heavy tidings of vengeance had not yet come. How wisely the Lord selected His words, not merely to warn, but to woo and win. When the national leaders classified Him as one of those who kept company with women who had sold their honor, and men of marred reputation, He replied: "I came not to call the righteous, but sinners to repentance" (Luke 5:32). His appeal rings out unsurpassed to this present hour, "Come unto Me, all ye that labour and are heavy laden, and I will give you rest" (Matt. 11:28). Never man preached and pleaded and pardoned as He did. He had not departed from this world but a few minutes when, to prove His loving interest, He sent His angel messengers with more thrilling news: "This same Jesus which is taken up from you into heaven, shall so come in like manner as ye have seen Him go into heaven" (Acts 1:11). Had He not said while with them, "I will come again and receive you unto Myself " (John 14:3)?

But in addition to the good news He Himself brought to man, He has sent word concerning things to come, and communicated the news to John on Patmos. His final message makes it possible for us to visualize the ascendency of His authority which reveals His ability to vindicate the righteousness of His cause, and vanquish the rebellion of evil forever. This is noteworthy news indeed, for it describes a tombless paradise, a realm of tearless perfection, and a sphere of thornless pleasure in a nightless day of fadeless light. A kingdom is portrayed in which the trials of toil are terminated, and the thrill of real reward expressed in trophies of honorable triumph greets the souls of His servants. Everlasting joy is jubilant in praise, and is realized in all the plenitude of divine fullness by virtue of the glorious victory of the Lamb. Perfected peace prevails over a scene of permanent grandeur, righteousness is regnant in sublimest splendor, and hope is honored and upheld in holiness forever.

The One who wore the sufferer's crown of sorrow on His brow when manifest in this world is now coronated with the crown of supernatural sovereignty. The One who bore the gladiator's garland of grief in His conflict with lawlessness is now adorned with the scintillating garland of glory. He, who won the warrior's wreath in righteous war against wickedness when "He was wounded for our transgressions," is now honored with the amaranthine wreath of worthiness. Yea, He is unveiled as having conquered the foe completely, and is crowned with the Christly coronet of conquest, which is one of the many diadems on His majestic head (Rev. 19:12). This magnificent spectacle so graphically portrayed was sent forth by Heaven's number one newscaster, Christ Jesus the Lord, who announces to us a description of the coming social order as being a faultless unison, a perfect harmony and a complete unity.

THE NUMBERER

He telleth the number of the stars; He calleth them all by their names. Great is our Lord, and of great power: His understanding is infinite (Ps. 147:4-5).

But the very hairs of your head are all numbered (Matt. 10:30).

God hath numbered thy kingdom, and finished it (Dan. 5:26).

And the number of the army of the horsemen were two hundred thousand thousand [i.e. two hundred million] and I heard the number of them (Rev. 9:16).

One of the clearly defined and most interesting and invaluable offices of Christ in Scripture revelation is indicated in this title, the Numberer. Sir William Herschel, the physicist and astronomer, was in the habit of saying: "This physical universe is so constructed that it is well nigh impossible to study any relative branch of science without a knowledge of mathematics." One other thing is equally true in this present creation, man is aware there are distances incalculable, dimensions inconceivable, dispositions inestimable, and durations incomprehensible to the natural mind. But the Son of God, the Creator, tells the number of the stars and knows the sands which are on the seashore innumerable, and has comprehended the dust of the earth in a measure.

If the measurements of material things are beyond the range of human reckoning, what are we to say of the spiritual realms so invisible to the human eye? Mathematical features of calculation which are so important in relation to the present order are entirely impotent in estimating celestial things. The manifold glories that emanate from Christ belong to a province where arithmetic has no sway, mathematics no sovereignty, and physics no sceptor. In contemplation of the ineffable, we read such expressions as "surpasseth knowledge," "unsearchable riches," "exceeding abundantly above all," "higher than the heavens," "the ages of the ages." All such terms suggest that which is undefinable. The self-illuminating gases which form the sun's chromosphere cannot be discerned apart from the spectroscope; then what have we as an aid for discerning the infinities of the infinite Christ?

He who tells the number of the stars stated plainly, "The very hairs of your head are all numbered." Said an old man with a half-bald pate, as he pointed to his head, during an address in a London congregation: "Does He count mine?"

The speaker promptly answered: "No, my friend. He knows; He is omniscient."

The Lord commanded Moses on two occasions to number Israel, not for His own information, but in order to impart

instruction. Over six hundred thousand from twenty years old
and upward paid the required levy, and four tons of precious
silver were used to make the sockets of the Tabernacle foundation to signify the cost of redemption, which the prophet declared is without price, that is, of priceless worth.

Even the celebrated Strauss, a noted pantheist, was compelled
to recognize these illustrious values and wrote in one of his latest
books: "Through the doctrine of atonement, the desolate feeling that we are the victims of chance vanishes before the sheltering arms of providence, and the darkness of the gloomy night
of our earthly life is illumined by the prospect of an immortal
and heavenly blessedness."

In that very Tabernacle, the pattern of which was revealed by
the Lord to Moses when on the mount, every loop and tache,
each curtain and covering, each pin and cord, each board and
brass coupling was numbered. One section of the Pentateuch in
the Old Testament bears the title, "The Book of Numbers," in
which the words *number* and *numbered* occur over one hundred
times. The One who names every family in earth and Heaven
also numbers every sheep in the flock of God and every soul in
the household of faith. He tabulates carefully, and keeps correctly the records of all the transactions of time; of everyday events,
from a falling sparrow to a feeling of sorrow, as well as keeping
the archives of national events. In the light of this we all need
to take heed to the prayer of Moses, the man of God, who
prayed, "So teach us to number our days that we may apply our
hearts unto wisdom." My personal toll of days has exceeded
twenty-five thousand and for at least twenty-two thousand of
these an account must be rendered. Job recognized the reality
of the great Numberer, and said of man, "Seeing his days are
determined, the number of his months are with Thee, Thou hast
appointed his bounds that he cannot pass" (Job 14:5). The message that was written by a mysterious hand on the wall of
Belshazzar's banqueting hall in Babylon, stated: "God hath numbered thy kingdom, and finished it" (Dan. 5:26). If Belshazzar
was condemned for contempt of God's claims, then what a

choice portion must be in reserve for those who seek to conform to His will.

In the Psalms it is written, "He healeth the broken in heart, and bindeth up their wounds. He telleth the number of the stars; He calleth them all by their names. Great is our Lord, and of great power: His understanding is infinite" (Ps. 147:3-5).

He who in His omniscience knows the number of the stars, understands also the griefs of every brokenhearted sufferer, and how many there are of such, needing His comfort. Our Saviour communicated to John that there were two hundred million angels round about the throne, and two hundred million horsemen in the army opposed to the advance of righteousness (Rev. 5:11; 9:16) besides the fact of the host of redeemed ones that exceeded all standards of human calculation and measures of reckoning. "A multitude no man could number." These staggering statements demand an infinite intelligence with absolute ability to account for everything and everyone, in both the visible and invisible universe. Advertisements appear in book catalogs from time to time offering works which are commended as being "a complete life of Christ." Can any writer compile a complete life of One who is from everlasting to everlasting, whom the Heaven of heavens cannot contain, who dwelleth in light which no man can approach, and the effulgence of whose eternal glory enlightened the sanctuary of the heavens before the world was?

How impressively grand is the portraiture of the radiant form and resolute feature of the illustrious Son of man in His replete fullness, as He is depicted in the Scriptures of truth. His magnificent ministries and munificent mercies are matchless and memorable. His mouth was untainted with the blame and shame of deceit and His motive untarnished with the smear and fear of sin. He uttered the greatest, deepest, loftiest thoughts that were ever spoken in this world. The years of His dignified ministry during the manifestation were devoted entirely to diffusing the sunshine of Heaven's deathless love and dispensing the boundless blessings of His Father's beneficient will. He abides eternally excellent in beauty, perfect in purity, complete in constancy, absolute in authority, matchless in majesty, supernal in sovereignty, and grandest in glory.

THE NOBLEMAN

And Jesus said unto him, This day is salvation come to this house, forsomuch as he also is a son of Abraham. For the Son of man is come to seek and to save that which was lost. And as they heard these things, He added and spake a parable, because He was nigh to Jerusalem, and because they thought that the kingdom of God should immediately appear. He said therefore, A certain nobleman went into a far country to receive for himself a kingdom, and to return. And he called his ten servants, and delivered them ten pounds, and said unto them, Occupy till I come (Luke 19:9-13).

In every realm of noble distinction Christ is most noble. He is worthily notable in His excellence of grace, and illustriously imposing in the effulgence of His glory, wherefore in all spheres of celebrity, dignity, and nobility He excels.

His nobility is perfectly expressed in mind and will and heart. An investigation of His credentials reveals that His knowledge was complete and full-orbed, for He said, "No one knows the Father save the Son." The will He expressed was sovereign and absolute which enabled Him to say, "I came not to do Mine own will, but the will of Him that sent Me," and again, "I do always those things that please Him." In meekness of heart He exhibited the might of God harnessed in human form to minister to men, and so He affirmed, "I and my Father are One."

These three features declare the knowledge of God, the kingdom of God, and the kindness of God as demonstrated in the Person of Jesus Christ the Lord, who is noblest of all nobility. These essential characteristics signify that in the consciousness of comprehension, in the completeness of cooperation, and in the comeliness of communion, Father and Son are One: A Oneness which He prayed might enrich and ennoble the people of

God (John 17:21). Surely nothing is more ennobling than one-ness of mind, will, and heart, in the eternal purpose of Heaven.

The significant occasion on which Christ used the designation "nobleman" is of great interest. When approaching the city of Jericho, Bartimaeus had loudly voiced his appeal by using the title, "Jesus, Thou Son of David." Within the city itself the chief tax collector Zacchaeus had attracted attention and publicly acknowledged Christ as Lord. The Saviour had addressed this wealthy man with commanding authority. He did not give utterance to any plaintive request as of a suppliant, but to the powerful resolve of a Sovereign, "Today I must abide at thy house."

The very atmosphere had grown tense with expectation and high hopes had been kindled among the populace. Many expected the kingdom of God would immediately appear in some dramatic form of material splendor. This surging state of mind drew forth from Christ the parable concerning a nobleman, who, on the eve of his departure to a distant country to receive a kingship, had called his ten servants and distributed to them ten pounds, urging them to occupy and maintain his interests until he returned.

The Lord used material that was common knowledge among the people. Not many years before, Herod went to Rome and was declared a king by the senate before Antigonus, through the influence of Antony. His son, Archelaus, was never received as king by the people, who had grown weary of the rule of the Herods. However, he built a palace not far from Jericho, and the members of the deputation that had gone to Rome to object to Archelaus being sanctioned jurisdiction were summarily arrested and executed.

In the light of what had transpired as a background, Christ indicated that He was about to proceed to a higher court than that of Rome for His investiture and that no amount of organized opposition would prevent His receiving complete administrative authority. Nor did He minimize the eventual outcome of what His coronation would mean to those who attempted to resist His rightful power. Before the end of the chapter, He foretold what He foresaw impending and predicted the over-throw of Jerusalem and destruction of the Temple. Obviously, the disciples themselves had not relished His teaching which had so discouraged the false anticipations of the populace, for it had also definitely dampened their aspirations as well.

Soon afterward He said to His disciples, "Verily I say to you, That ye which have followed Me, in the regeneration when the Son of man shall sit in the throne of His glory, ye also shall sit upon twelve thrones judging the twelve tribes of Israel" (Matt. 19:28). The expression "regeneration" suffices to show that the constitution of the kingdom is not one that pertains to the present generation of humanity, but belongs to a new order, the generation of Jesus Christ.

When the Lord first commissioned His disciples and en-trusted them with His interests, His words of advice covered three phases of the task, as Dr. G. Campbell Morgan points out in his exposition of Matthew's Gospel.

The first characterized the three-and-a-half-year period of His earthly ministry while He was present with them. The second aspect ranged from the time of His ascension until the destruc-tion of Jerusalem and the Temple. The third period extended from the desolation of Jerusalem until the second advent. In relation to the second of these He said, "Ye shall not have gone over the cities of Israel, till the Son of man be come" (Matt. 10:23). Christ was just as really present supervising the destruc-tion of Jerusalem in A.D. 70, as He was present superintending the destruction of the firstborn in Egypt, on which occasion He said, "When I see the blood I will pass over you." How clearly He depicted and described the overthrow (Matt. 22:7).

In the deepest sense and fullest meaning of the word, Christ is the most distinguished nobleman of the centuries. Yea, His nobility is clearly expressed in the highest dignity of human life, in the grandest majesty of heavenly love, and in the divinest reality of holy Lordship. He was always characterized by a virtue devoid of any vulnerable point whatever, and was possessed of a disposition wholly free from the slightest degree of deficiency or defect of any kind. His noble nature was entirely immune from parochial narrowness and national pride. Christ stands out conspicuously as the chief Prince of regality, the King of all royalty, the Lord of all majesty, the Head of all celebrity, the Master of all excellency, the Governor of all authority, and the most Notable of all nobility. When He had passed through the processes of manifestation, ministrations, crucifixion, resurrection, and ascension, the celestial courts were wide open to His rightful claim and His course was clear, as it is written, "Ask of Me, and I shall give Thee the heathen for Thine inheritance, and the uttermost parts of the earth for Thy possession" (Ps. 2:8).

The Father hath now given all things into His hands. We must needs consider that Christ, who is the embodiment of true nobility, has a definite design in His delegation and distribution of bounty. The main objective is to develop character and test integrity and loyalty, and also prove the capacity and industry of each servant. Whatever bestowment He makes of the graces, talents, pounds, and abilities at His disposal, the sole purpose He has in mind is with a view to future honor. At His return He will fully compensate the fidelity and energy of His servants and confer additional authority on all work that warrants it. The biggest bonuses, the largest legacies, the repletest revenues are to be derived from trading in the moral and spiritual realities that constitute the kingdom interests of this noble and notable royal Master.

The entrustment and endowment He imparts to each severally as He wills should make us eagerly expectant of the vaster things yet to be expressed and established on that victorious day, when the glorious Victor Himself, shall return to review and reward the stewardship of His faithful servants.

The superiority of Christ in the category we are considering is strikingly verified in an incident recorded by John. A nobleman of the court of Herod Antipas was impelled through love for his son, who was seriously ill, to venture to come to Christ as a last resort for help. Under the shadow of threatened bereavement, and in deep agony of soul, he said, "Sir, come down, ere my child die." Christ responded to this imperial demand, with an imperative command, "Go, for thy son liveth." Astonished, but assured, with the presence and personality of a greater nobility, the nobleman went his way.

The sterling excellence of Christ's supreme nobility is evidenced in His unceasing deployment of knowledge, in His unending dominion of Kingship, and in His undying disposition of kindness. The spaciousness of His majesty and the graciousness of His mastery constitute a profound mystery which shall not be clarified until we see Him face to face.

THE NOBLE NEGOTIATOR

And their nobles shall be of themselves, and their governor shall proceed from the midst of them; and I will cause him to draw near, and he shall approach unto Me: for who is this that engaged his heart to approach unto Me? saith the Lord (Jer. 30:21).

Now the God of peace, that brought again from the dead our Lord Jesus, that great shepherd of the sheep, through the blood of the everlasting covenant, Make you perfect in every good work to do His will (Heb. 13:20-21).

The terms "noble," "nobles," and "most noble," appear over fifty times in the Old Testament and the word is used to describe persons of excellent disposition who are dignified, stately, and honorable in their uprightness. The Revised Version in this case renders the word "prince." On the other hand, a negotiator is one who secures an agreement with another, or one that procures by mutual consent, a peace settlement, considered to be of real value to others, and of lasting worth. In this essential function also, Christ is nonpareil, yea, He is *facile princeps,* that is, without equal and admittedly chief. In His great contract of mediating the everlasting covenant (which is the subject of Jeremiah 30—33, and through which a peace that passeth understanding and a love that surpasseth knowledge is secured), and in view of His grand constancy as the Reconciler of man back into divine favor, Christ is the most noble of all negotiators. This stupendous undertaking required one of outstanding caliber that was beyond compare in character and nobility, and without reproach in conduct and integrity. Christ never once dishonored the reputation of deity in holiness of purpose, nor digressed in any wise from the pure path of rectitude in righteousness of practice. After negotiating the terms of agreement in consort with the eternal Father, He came and confirmed the covenant to mankind, and conveyed, to all those who believe, the blessed assurance that iniquity, transgression, and sin have been expunged and the power of death nullified.

In negotiating the compact, the supreme factor in the terms of the contract required His own vicarious death, wherefore He offered His virtuous life in substitutionary sacrifice, and by virtue of His victorious resurrection, vindicated the righteous justice of God and verified the sanction of justification for man. The sequel of this glorious accomplishment assures us that He has become the author of eternal salvation to all them that obey Him (Heb. 5:9).

The Son of man, the Saviour, is therefore the all-sufficient solution of the supremest problem that confronts the human mind. How can guilty man be just, or justified before God? That is, made perfectly righteous in His sight. Christ is the sole and sufficient answer to the question. He declares the divine claims fully, He disposes of all difficulties perfectly, He dispenses God's mercy abundantly, He delivers the ensnared entirely, He defeats all enemies completely, He determines to make all things new absolutely, and He designs all such activities for the glory of God eternally.

Every competent, unprejudiced judge, who has examined the gospel records, is prepared to admit that Christ in manifestation realized the perfect ideal of manhood. Then, may we ask, what was the inner secret of this? Was it not His supreme recognition of holding a right relationship to God in everything? He declared, in His teaching to His disciples, God's knowledge of man: "the Father knoweth that ye have need." He affirmed God's love for man: "The Father Himself loveth you." He assured God's rule for man: "Seek ye first the kingdom of God." And He attested God's interest in man, "If God so clothe the grass of the field [with so many delicate tints and textures] will He not much more clothe you?" Christ accumulated assurances and blended them with a selection of supernatural signs to stimulate confidence and secure ceaseless consolation for trusting souls. His words had a wider horizon, His works a worthier purpose, and His ways were of weightier significance than any previously known to man. The evidences of His inner excellence were expressed in the truth He taught, in the works He wrought, and in the goal He sought, which kept prominently in view the glorifying of the name of the Most High.

His manners, too, were always serene and He showed the choicest courtesy which was indicative of high rank. The means He used were the best possible, and the most suitable, yea, superfine to a degree which reflected His noble nature. The blessings He bestowed were sublime and exhibited the innermost quality of His divine character.

Christ had a crystal-clear conception of all commencements and consummations, a complete comprehension of the celestial and eternal realities, and a consciousness which was characterized by an awareness of all circumstances and existing conditions. The Scriptures repeatedly define the perfect and describe the ineffable by using the negative form of expressions, for instance, the glory of the inheritance is indescribable, and therefore, we are told of the nonexisting characteristics, namely, incorruptible, undefiled, and unfading. Then again, in a more lengthy description, we are told there are no thorns, no tears, no trials, no pain, and no death in that domain. This method, when adopted in relation to the incomparable Christ, is suggestive, for there was nothing forced or artificial about Him at any time, nothing strained or nonsensical, nothing crude or hypocritical, nothing rude or unethical, nothing mean or whimsical, nothing false or hysterical, and nothing vulgar or satirical. On the positive side, the balance of perfect equipoise characterized

Him always, so that the beauty of His demeanor and the burnish of His deportment were a demonstration of excellence excelled. We may say emphatically our blessed Lord ennobled nobility, He endowed dignity, He enriched regality, He enlarged liberality, and He engraced glory. He Himself is the sum and substance of superiority in everything, everywhere, and everlastingly.

THE NEIGHBOR

Awake, O sword, against My shepherd, and against the man that is My neighbour, [rendered fellow in AV] saith the Lord of Hosts (Zech. 13:7).

Who is my neighbour? . . . Which now of these three, thinkest thou, was neighbour unto him that fell among the thieves? And he said, That which showed mercy on him (Luke 10:29, 36-37).

We are all familiar with the common idea that a neighbor is one who lives next door, but a lesson in geography by no means exhausts the idea. One who lives right alongside your home may be anything but neighborly. A true neighbor is one in the same vicinity who shows a friendly spirit and offers a helping hand whatever the need. In the case Christ cited, the certain man to whom He referred and the Samaritan may never have seen each other before. But the Samaritan was in a position to meet the existing need, was disposed to help the stricken man, and readily did so.

Two others were in the vicinity, a priest and a Levite. Maybe at that very time they were wearing the livery of the Temple of Jerusalem and knew how to recite its liturgies, but failed in the neighborly function of befriending a needy soul and let him lie and sigh and, for that matter, die. The Samaritan to whom Christ referred made no excuses, nor did he blame the excesses of demands on his time as a reason for not assisting, but expressed the kindly care and considerate pity which the case required. How consoling it becomes on the highway of life to meet a nice neighbor who takes in the whole situation at a glance and who lavishes attention and aid ungrudgingly and without stint.

The greatest Neighbor known is the One we all need most and He is not far from any one of us, for "in Him we live, and move, and have our being" (Acts 17:28). He is nigh unto all who call upon Him, wherefore:

> Speak to Him, thou, for He hears,
>   And spirit and spirit may meet,
> Closer is He than breathing,
>   And nearer than hands or feet.

One hundred and eighty references to the word "neighbor" occur in the Old Testament. The relationship was incorporated in the Ten Commandments of the Law. "Thou shalt love thy neighbour as thyself," and Christ taught that this requirement was second only in importance to loving God with all the heart and mind and strength. The word rendered "fellow" in Zechariah 13:7 is the same as that which is translated "neighbour" ten times in the book of Leviticus. See for example Leviticus 25:14. He who is God's neighbor, is also neighbor to me, for the Lord laid our help upon one that is mighty.

Christ, by His teaching and example, stimulated self-abnegating service, and self-denying sacrifice on behalf of others. Neighborly qualities of the truest character were expressed in His real friendship and reliable faithfulness. How lovingly and loyally He ministered to those overtaken by adversity. The Gospel of John supplies a graphic account of the manner in which Christ proved to be a genuine neighbor to Andrew in His yearning desire to have the sin problem solved, to the master of ceremonies in his dilemma at a wedding banquet, to the disquieted mind of a man of the Pharisees, to the disaffected heart of a Samaritan woman, to the distress of a nobleman over his son's illness, to a defiled woman in the temple courts accused of impurity, to the sisters of Bethany when death had removed their beloved brother, to Peter the denier, and to Thomas the doubter.

Yea, in every case of dire need, when the heart craved for relief, He proved a true lover and stood hard by with copious comfort and conspicuous care to lighten the burden and lift the load from the downcast. We may all live and enjoy the conscious nearness of this never-failing Neighbor, who is always strong and sympathetic with adequate ability to succor, and is never weary in welldoing. He is genuinely great and graciously generous, ready at all times to rescue and restore. In His thoughtful tenderness, He is ever mindful and merciful in dealing with the distressed and defeated. Christ is the neighbor of all nations and nigh unto everyone in the whole realm of humanity. Therefore, because He is intimately related as the Son of man, and infinitely fitted as the Son of God, He is perfectly qualified to fulfill this familiar function of neighbor toward all men, everywhere.

In one of the suburbs of the capital city of Queensland, Australia, there lived a well-known Sunday school teacher named Blanchard. He had an extensive area of ground surrounding his home and had planted a portion of it in fruit trees, besides keeping a well-cultivated vegetable garden. The adjacent residence fell vacant, and after a time a new tenant rented the place. The man from the outset appeared gruff, cantankerous, and unfriendly. Some weeks after his arrival there was a heavy downpour of rain and the Blanchards were astonished to find leaks in every room of their home. An investigation revealed that someone had been on their roof and had cracked a number of their tiles.

On another occasion, when they returned from a day's outing they discovered that all the fruit trees in the orchard had been ring-barked, which meant their total loss. New difficulties were arising continually, and one day two detectives arrived at the Blanchard home with a warrant to search the house because the person living next door had accused them of stealing his ax and other articles. They were now fully aware of the one who was damaging their property and seeking to injure their reputation.

After two years of such experiences they noticed the local doctor's car parked in front of the house next door and upon making inquiry, learned that the troublemaker was ill with cancer, and no longer able to work. Mr. Blanchard asked his wife to ascertain what kind of food had been ordered for the sick man. On being informed that he could have egg custard, milk puddings, and soups, Mrs. Blanchard made an errand daily to help minister to the requirements.

One day, to her surprise, the wife said her husband wished to see Mr. Blanchard. Nothing was so unexpected. The doctor had said another month would see the matter through. That same evening when Mr. Blanchard entered the sick room the patient began sobbing bitterly. "Is the pain excessive tonight?" he enquired.

"It's not that," said the sick man. "For the past two years I have done all in my power to aggravate you and to damage your property. I cracked tiles on your roof, I ring-barked your fruit trees, I stole your vegetables, and in return have received nothing but kindness. I can't understand it."

Mr. Blanchard thereupon explained to him the why of it all, and said he had done what he could for His Saviour's sake. He then told him of Christ's love and all it had meant to him through life, and eventually led the sick man to repentance and faith in the Lord Jesus.

The weeks elapsed and nightly Blanchard would slip in for a few minutes, read a psalm and pray with him. The doctor then told the sick man it would be necessary to see to arrangements for the funeral, as death was at the door. "What minister would you like us to call?"

He answered faintly, "I do not want a minister to conduct the burial service. None ever came near me. I want the man next door to do it. He was the only one who cared for my soul." Blanchard had proved a real neighbor to the stricken man and expressed to him the same gracious kindness that he himself had experienced from that wonderful neighbor, the Son of man.

What a mercy that the Father of lights, with whom is no variableness, sent us the Son of man to be a constant Comrade, a gracious Guide, a faithful Friend, a close Companion, a kindly Kinsman, and an abiding Associate, all of which are summed up in the supernatural Neighbor who is ever at hand to assist and assure, a very present help in time of trouble.

His tender touch, His loving look, His helping hand, His constant care, reassure the drooping heart by engendering fresh hope, by encouraging free access, and by enlarging faith's vision. What a Neighbor!

THE NAZARENE

And He came and dwelt in a city called Nazareth: that it might be fulfilled which was written by the prophets, He shall be called a Nazarene (Matt. 2:23).

One of the important factors in the divine purpose Christ came to unfold was that of acquainting man with the real seat of rule and authority. In the discharge of His commission He did not direct attention to military might, but to mediatorial mercy, as being of supreme importance. His chief concern was not centered in armament and resourceful supplies, but in salvation and remission of sins. His system of teaching did not include lectures on strategic skill, but was concerned with the fundamental principle of substitutionary sacrifice.

These things are far more essential in the establishment of perfect government than any other items. We might have expected that Christ would have made this aspect of His mission arrestingly impressive by a dignified birthplace, not a cattle stall; a distinguished boyhood, not one centered in a carpenter's work room; and by living in a distinctive metropolis, not in the most contemptible town in Galilee. No human would have chosen such humble stations as stepping-stones to the seat of highest honor, or as a means of ascent to the supreme summit of supernal glory. But Christ was never lacking in one single feature of royal rank, sovereign strength, regal right, or moral might during the whole period of His earthly manifestation. He did not borrow anything of His excellent name and enduring fame from the peoples and places of this world. The palatial home, the private school, the prominent university, made no contribution to His perfect knowledge and preeminent Kingship. The light of His unlit radiance glows effulgently to this very hour because the entire entity of His personality is eternal.

Let us notice some of the accredited ideas that were commonly attached to the town of Nazareth, a town which had been placed under the jurisdiction of the Herods, whose voluptuous habits had made the place utterly unwholesome. The answer

Nathanael gave to Philip throws a flood of light on existing estimates. Philip emphasized that the prophet of age-old renown, whom Moses had predicted was to come to teach all things, had actually arisen in Nazareth. To this statement Nathanael replied, "Can there any *good* thing come out of Nazareth?"

Philip answered, "Come and see."

Years ago a construction firm in London that had been plunged into financial difficulties sued an engineering company for heavy damages. They were endeavoring to cover up their own breach of contract by placing the blame on a flywheel that had been cast for the machinery of a weaving mill they were erecting, having sublet the contract for the flywheel to a nearby firm. Unknown to the claimants, the engineers had had the rejected wheel brought to the proximity of the courtroom where the case was being tried. At the decisive moment during the proceedings when the presiding judge asked the lawyer for the defense if he had anything to counter the serious charge that had just been made, he answered "Your honor, and gentlemen of the jury, *come and see* the wheel in question at the rear of the court." When the attendants had removed the covering from the large object, the lawyer said, "Gentlemen, there's the wheel." It was such a splendid piece of engineering skill the case was decided in favor of the accused.

"Come and see" is all that is necessary to convince an interested soul that the One described is greater in distinction than any advocate of His claims is capable of declaring. So far as Nazareth was concerned, it was a place that could be conveniently ignored without imperiling the commercial interests of trade or the cultural benefits of learning. Therefore the locality was not considered a likely center from whence one would arise who was destined to fill an important role in relation to history, prophecy, or society. The origin of the name may have been derived from the old Hebrew word *Netzer,* which means a shoot, sprout, stem, or even branch. When a sucker springs up from a stump it lacks the symmetry and beauty of a tree growing on its original trunk. This feature appears to be the real significance of the use that is made of the word in the present case. Isaiah,

Jeremiah, and others of the prophets foretold the cutting off of the kingdom of Israel. The Assyrian power is likened to a cedar being cut down, which never sprouts again (Isa. 10). The nation of Israel is spoken of as a teil tree or an oak, which, if cut down, shoots again, and in this case the holy seed is to be the substance thereof (Isa. 6:11-13).

Later, the prophet declared that a rod would come forth out of the stem of Jesse and a branch grow out of his roots, one whose inner motives and outer ministries would be engirdled by faithfulness and righteousness (Isa. 11:1-5). Christ claimed to be the root of verse ten, in His final declaration to John (Rev. 22:16). The profound importance of these statements is clarified by those wonderful words, "Who hath believed our report? and to whom is the arm of the Lord revealed? For He shall grow up before Him as a tender plant and as a shoot out of a dry root" (Isa. 53:1-2 Dr. A. McLaren's rendering).

Also Jeremiah in his profound chapters on the covenant uses the word *Netzer* in reference to Christ, "In those days, and at that time, will I cause the *Branch* of righteousness to grow up into David" (Jer. 33:15). Disguised in lowly mien, and disrobed of the outward appearance and radiance of heavenly glow, Christ grew up in the obscure and despised town of Nazareth. But He needed no physical grandeur in His surroundings to make Him great. He required no political patronage to make Him famous. He desired no provincial recognition to promote His intrinsic royalty. Inherently, our Saviour possessed an excellence wholly independent of national environment. His sterling sovereignty did not rely on stately surroundings for its superior distinction. His dignified majesty was not engendered by the multitudes, nor by millions in monetary wealth.

As in all other relationships, so in this sphere also, the unique personality of Christ stands out in clear relief, for He is not dependent for His renown on any creature or community, nor does His nobility rely on the greatness of any famous character or familiar city. His contact with all such served to bring into clearer light His inherent moral glory which was wholly underived and entirely unconferred. Christ's status in no sense rests upon human honor or relies on material splendor, either for its existence or maintenance. He imparts to all others their dignity and desirability but never derives any such qualities from anyone. Therefore His period of residence in the proverbial city of Nazareth neither developed in any form, nor detracted in any feature whatsoever, from His moral attributes and majestic authority.

The calm dignity which He always expressed clearly displayed the regal distinction of His imperial character, while the composed deportment He consistently exhibited, disclosed the real dominion of His celestial nature. If we reflect back over the whole range of revealed truth, no one is more lustrous in prophecy, more famous in history, more gracious in majesty, more precious in ministry, more generous in mercy, more wondrous in chivalry, more spacious in authority, or more glorious in eternity, than the Christ of God.

O

The fully qualified Saviour is strong to support and powerful to sustain His people. His capacities, capabilities, and competencies are completely efficient, and He is almighty to subdue all the opposing powers of evil.

The OFFERING (Eph. 5:2; Heb. 10:10)
> The Offering that outweighs and outranges all the demands of justice.

The OFFSPRING OF DAVID (Rev. 22:16)
> The Originator and Overseer of all regents and righteous rule.

The OVERCOMER (Rev. 3:21; 17:14)
> The most virtuous of victors, preeminent in prevailing triumph.

The ONLY-BEGOTTEN (John 1:18; 3:16)
> The foremost and final Declarer and Demonstrator of deity.

The OMNIPOTENT ONE (Jer. 32:17; Rev. 19:6-7)
> The strongest in ability and authority who surpasses in grace and mercy.

The OMNISCIENT ONE (Isa. 46:9-10; John 2:24; Heb. 4:13)
> The mind of infinite intelligence and unlimited insight.

The OMNIPRESENT ONE (Ps. 139:4-12)
> The everpresent Shepherd who is available always, everywhere.

The OFFERER (Heb. 9:24-25; 10:12)
> The most suitable and acceptable who offered Himself.

The ONLY WISE GOD (1 Tim. 1:17)
> The Creator, Redeemer, Sustainer, and Perfecter.

153

The OWL OF THE DESERT (Ps. 102:6)

    The solitary Sufferer who defeated the powers of darkness.

The ORACLE OF GOD (John 8:26; 12:49; Heb. 1:1)

    The exact expression of everlasting truth.

The OMEGA (Rev. 22:13)

    The focus and finality of the stream of faith and sea of fullness.

THIS IS THE NAME WHEREBY HE SHALL BE CALLED THE LORD OUR RIGHTEOUSNESS

> *His righteousness never recedes*
> *His loving-kindness never lessens*
> *His faithfulness never fails*
> *His comeliness never ceases*
> *His delightfulness never dwindles*
> *His preciousness never perishes*
> *His steadfastness never subsides*
> *His worthiness never wanes*

THY NAME IS FROM EVERLASTING

Lord of the everlasting Name
Whose works proclaim eternal fame,
Thy love and mercy far exceed
The utmost depths of human need.

Omnipotent in power and might
With every claim of sovereign right,
Yet there is none Thou wilt despise
Nor disregard the prayers that rise.

Of righteousness and truth the spring,
In highest majesty the King,
But mindful of the lost and lone,
Dispensing mercy from Thy throne.

In perfect holiness arrayed,
With everlasting love portrayed,

Thy kindly deeds of help and grace,
Are shown to all who seek Thy face.

The eternal grandeur of Thy Name
In changeless character the same,
Invites the weary sons of earth,
To take the gift of priceless worth.

C.J.R.

I am Alpha and Omega (Rev. 22:13)

Christ is the loneliest character in history, for there is none like Him, so that He is without compare (Isa. 40:18). He is the loveliest personality known, for in every characteristic He is absolutely perfect (S. of Sol. 5:16). He is the loftiest being of the highest heavenly hierarchy, the Lord of lords and God of gods. Following the enthronement of His excellency at the right hand of God, He expressed Himself as God's Alphabet, the Alpha and Omega, which constitutes in its significance that He is the veritable key of all abiding wisdom and spiritual knowledge. He also declared Himself to be God's Authority, the Beginning and the End, the very Door of destiny and the Entrance to eternal salvation. He likewise affirmed Himself to be God's Arithmetic, the First and Last, the Source, Sum, and Substance of all spiritual sufficiency to the utmost degree.

Wherever we view Him, His life is lustrous with "the light of the knowledge of the glory of God" (2 Cor. 4:6), and He is forever adorned in the beauteous garment of godlike goodness. In the highest distinction of divine resemblance and relationship, He reflects the glorious likeness of the Father as the Son of God (John 14:9), for the magnificence of eternal deity is reflected in the beloved Son. By the very constituency of His celestial nature, His gracious deportment fully expresses the very image of God's personality (Heb. 1:3). By virtue of His love of righteousness and hatred of iniquity, He sways the imperishable scepter of supreme sovereignty from the eternal throne of God (Heb. 1:8).

In harmony with the perfect peace He established by His Cross, He is our peace (Eph. 2:14), and demonstrates in His perfectly balanced character the peace of God (Phil. 4:7). In the unassailable activity of His commanding authority, in quelling storms, quenching the fiery darts of the wicked one, and quickening the dead, He fully exhibited the power of God (1 Cor. 1:24). When at last the final conflict rages, in righteousness He will make war, and as a tribute of justice emblazoned on His thigh, He rides forth with a name written thereon, "The Word of God" (Rev. 19:11,13). Ultimate issues are altogether under the sway of His unbounded control, for He made that unprecedented declaration to the Apostle John on Patmos, "Behold, I make all things new. . . . Write: for these words are true and faithful" (Rev. 21:5).

With the innumerable qualifications He holds in positions of noblest dignity and highest distinction, He is perfectly equipped in ability to succor the tempted, sustain the tried, and save to the uttermost. We should bear in mind that every effectual resource for achieving redemption, every essential requisite for accomplishing reconciliation and every eternal repleteness for administering recreation resides and remains in the hands of Christ Jesus, our blessed Lord and Saviour. Let us revel and rejoice in the revealed knowledge that in every summit of supremacy, in every circuit of sovereignty, in every orbit of sanctity, and in every degree of superiority, Christ stands supreme. We now turn in our meditation to consider twelve of our Lord's names and titles commencing with the letter O.

THE OFFERING

Christ also hath loved us, and hath given Himself for us an offering and a sacrifice to God for a sweetsmelling savour (Eph. 5:2).

The offering of the body of Jesus Christ once for all (Heb. 10:10).

Concentration of thought on such an offering as this plunges the mind into a measureless sea of contemplation. We enter the realm of the inestimable and incalculable when we muse on an offering of such magnitude, which involves a person of such magnificent bearing and beauty. Christ is altogether too pure a character to be defiled as a sin offering, too perfect to be pained by grief, too great in pity to be persecuted by enemies, too loving to be scarred by a scourge, too full of tenderness to be torn with thorns, and too comely to be cursed by a cross of shame.

The offering of the body of Jesus Christ, which was so perfect because prepared by the Spirit of holiness, is an offering without price, including virtue that cannot be valued, involving worth that cannot be priced, and incorporating preciousness that can-not be determined. "Unto you therefore which believe He is the preciousness" (1 Pet. 2:7).

A supernal offering of such sort silences the serious demands of justice, settles the enormous debt of sin, secures the gracious dominion of mercy, satisfies the stupendous claims of righteous-ness, signifies the spacious love of God, and at the same time seals the dethronement of the devil and the doom of death.

We need reminding repeatedly that we are not redeemed with corruptible things such as silver and gold, "But with the precious blood of Christ, as of a lamb without blemish and without spot" (1 Pet. 1:19).

Another significant feature lies in the fact that this offering is the most fragrant ever presented, yea, the very sweetest, choic-est, purest, comeliest in character that was ever known, and for such an one to be placed upon an altar astounds the intellect and amazes the mind.

Who could conceive of One who is altogether lovely in dispo-sition, almighty in dominion, and all merciful in design, deign-ing to become an offering for sinners, the pure for the impure, the potent for the impotent, the perfect for the imperfect? The offering here portrayed and personified is the marvel of mar-vels, the miracle of miracles, and the mystery of mysteries, for there is no conceivable parallel to such a sacrifice throughout the annals of history. Never before had a person so generous in mercy, so gracious in ministry, and so glorious in majesty appeared among men. That such an One should become the expiatory offering for sin seems on first thought to be inconceivable. The ordinance which had reference to the character of the offering required under the old covenant stated, "it shall be perfect to be accepted; there shall be no blemish therein" (Lev. 22:21).

When the Only-begotten voluntarily offered Himself without spot to God in cheerful obedience to the divine will, He fulfilled this primary obligation which was ordained of God as the only acceptable oblation to justify man from guilt. Christ is a celebrity of such dignity of nature and of such character that if He be removed He cannot be replaced, He is the sole one of His kind, the only one of His class. None other is qualified for a perfect offering. Where in the whole wide world would we find another possessed of the same degree of distinction, the same rank of reputation, the same standard of superiority, the same measure of majesty, the same level of loving-kindness, the same scale of sovereignty, the same rule of righteousness, and a similar state of suitability for sacrifice, than the Christ of God? To those who have implicit faith in Christ as a personal Saviour, no theme can excel in virtue or exceed in value that of the vicarious sacrifice of Christ.

The justice of God must needs repel and repulse with infinite disgust those who refuse to avail of the blessings which so wondrous a sacrifice and so precious an offering secures. All Heaven resounds with the resonance of a new song which is sung by myriads and myriads in commemoration of the Redeemer's great conquest, which He won when clad in the battle dress of His sacrificial character as the Lamb that was slain (Rev. 5:6,9).

This scene impresses us with some idea of the infinite issues resulting from His redemptive work, and conveys a clearer comprehension of how virtuous is the sacrifice that He made, how vast the ransom that He paid, how valid the reason that He gave and how vital the victory that He gained.

He who is the essential essence of life, light, and love, the spring and stream of mercy, ministry, and majesty and the sum and substance of righteousness, goodness, and holiness, combined with every other attribute of deity, constitutes the offering presented. The descriptive details that are given of Christ in the four Gospels reflect and reveal the perfection of His full-orbed character and faultless conduct. How memorable His ministry, how lovable His majesty, how durable His constancy, how amiable His courtesy, how desirable His sympathy, how likeable His humility, how pleasurable His company, and how admirable His integrity! The reality of His dedication is unquestionable, the loyalty of His devotion is unimpeachable, while the royalty of His dominion is unchallengeable. In these virtues and in all other qualtities His surpassing excellence is undeniable. Such a dignified Person loved us, and hath given Himself for us an OFFERING and a sacrifice to God for a sweet-smelling savor. His wisdom devised it, His will determined it, His word declared it, and His work displayed it, for He finished the work the Father gave Him to do (John 17:4).

THE OFFSPRING OF DAVID

I Jesus have sent Mine angel to testify unto you these things in the churches. I am the root and the offspring of David, and the bright, the morning star (Rev. 22:16,RV).

In this, our Lord's last reference to His own majestic personality, He uses three figures of speech which signify His authorship, leadership, and governorship. When approaching the study of His matchless character, we discover that one of the main avenues of enlightenment on the subject is disclosed in the references He makes to the great leaders of the past. The Lord was fully aware of the renown of Abraham, the patriarch and progenitor of the Hebrew race, and exclaimed when challenged about His own age, "Before Abraham was born, I am" (John

8:58 margin). When questioned on the magnificence of resource exhibited by Moses to a nation for forty years, and in comparison the meagerness of the supply which He had furnished to a few thousand folk for one day, He replied, "I am the bread of life. Your fathers did eat manna in the wilderness and are dead, this is the bread which cometh down from heaven that a man may eat thereof and not die . . . he shall live forever" (John 6:31-35). The resource of Moses was limited to one nation, the resource of Christ is for the world (John 6:51).

On another occasion when Jewish leaders were discussing authorities on the subject of duty, destiny, and devotion, Christ imposed a simple question, "What think ye of Christ, whose son is He," knowing full well their answer would be linked with the most regal of their historic kings.

They replied, "The Son of David."

"Then," said He, "seeing David speaks of Messiah as 'My Lord,' how is He his son?"

When contention was rife over the subject of reputation and the rulers derided Him, He reminded them that Solomon's reputation spread to distant countries and constrained the Queen of Sheba to journey to Jerusalem to hear His wisdom, then He added, "behold, a greater than Solomon is here" (Matt. 12:42).

Christ Himself is the Instigator and Progenitor, the Originator and Maintainer of all these remarkable men, and is also the Author and Perfecter of their faith. The revenue He derives from their lives is in the form of the credit they contribute to the capabilities of His creatorship. The potter is praised by virtue of the precious porcelain vase he made. The artist is acclaimed because of the ability displayed in his masterpiece. The humanitarian is honored because of the wonderful help he has rendered to humanity. So Christ is worthy of worship in the light of His workmanship which is so wonderfully portrayed in the lives of these leaders. He formed and fashioned each one of them for a special part in His purpose, and their individual capacities and capabilities when fully perfected and combined in one personality, give us just a faint glimmer of the magnitude of His full-orbed completeness. In other words, all the renown of Abraham, the resourcefulness of Moses, the regality of David, the reputation of Solomon, and every other reputable character-istic of every soul in the galleries of the great through all time, is found in full bloom and perfect beauty in the immortal Christ, "For of Him, and through Him, and to Him, are all things" (Rom. 11:36).

Let us consider this celebrated claim, "I am the root and offspring of David, the bright, the morning star." The proclama-tion is profound beyond all telling. In the threefold form of the declaration we find indicated the supernatural distinction of Christ as the Root, His superior dominion as the Offspring of David, and His superlative designation as the Morning Star. These unusual titles depict Him as being the Originator of David's life, the Overseer of his reign, and the Overcomer of the dark-ness of death. Christ is anterior to David as the Ancient of Days, yea, the acknowledged Progenitor ever-abiding in ageless abili-ty, and is the very spring of David's life of trust.

Christ is superior to David as the Arm of the Lord, the Author and Arbiter of His sanctioned authority, who declares, "By Me kings reign and princes decree justice." Wherefore Christ is the source of David's leadership of triumph.

Moreover, our Shepherd-Saviour is the super-Sovereign, the Star of monarchs, the very King of kings, and Lord of lords in absolute administration, the sole supplier of David's light of truth. A survey of this triple title reveals that in His progenitor-ship as the Root, Christ is the Instigator of David's character, for He produced it. In proprietorship as his Offspring, He is the interpreter of David's career, for He planned it. In premiership as the Star, He is the inspirer of David's chivalry, for He pro-moted it. So we perceive that behind David's ancestry, authori-ty, and ability stands the Almighty Author, Arbiter, and Autocrat, Jesus Christ the Lord. We have used the word Autocrat with a set purpose in view of the Greek, *despotès,* being used of Christ on ten occasions in the New Testament.

Our Lord in this final statement of claim to John on Patmos

was laying stress on His divinity, durability, and deity and the figures He uses indicate that He holds the scepter of life, wears the miter of love, and sheds the luster of light eternally.

Let us look more closely at the central feature of the claim made, "I am . . . the offspring of David." We cannot do more than touch on three or four of the main lines of evidence for verification.

The New Testament speaks of Christ as Son of David in His identity with the tribe of Judah (Heb. 7:14); as being of the seed of David in His intimacy with the Hebrew race (John 7:42; Rom. 1:3; 2 Tim. 2:8); as of the city of David in His society with the Judean government (Luke 2:4; John 7:42); as of the house of David in His affinity with the royal line (Luke 1:69); as of the tabernacle of David in His ministry of mediation (Acts 15:16); as of the throne of David in His majesty, the sovereign Lord (Luke 1:32); as of the kingdom of David in His authority as supreme Administrator (Mark 11:10). Another score of such references is available, but these seven suffice to show the vital link in the lineage and to corroborate Christ's claim as being the Offspring of David.

Following these historical marks of identification, we shall select seven of the moral victories David gained alone and submit a similar number of far greater consequence in the life of Christ.

Notice first of all some of the interesting stages through which David passed from a state of mediocrity to maturity. He was ruddy as a lad, reliable as a shepherd, rigorous as a servant, resourceful as a fugitive, resolute as a leader, regal as a king, and righteous as a ruler. These qualities of character were supported and sustained by greater moral virtues, for he was a man of excellent spirit.

On the occasion when war broke out between Israel and Philistia, David was quite a lad and most of the vigorous young men were eager to go to the scene of the conflict, but David stayed by his flock and thereby gained a victory over inquisitiveness (1 Sam. 17:13-15). "He that ruleth his spirit [is better] than he that taketh a city" (Prov. 16:32). During the long hours in the open he did not idle his time away but taught himself to play several instruments and became the king's musician. By virtue of his diligence he gained the victory over indolence. Some weeks after the war started his father said to his son, "Take an ephah of parched corn and ten loaves to your brethren, and ten cheeses to their captain, and see how they fare." Surely this opportunity would cause David to vacate his existing task with all haste, but not so. He first sought out a keeper for his sheep, and in this matter gained the victory over indifference (1 Sam. 17:20).

Although he took this journey in the interests of his brethren, Eliab accused him of inquisitiveness and neglect (1 Sam. 17:28). David knew his brother well enough to have retaliated with incriminations of cowardice, but turned away and gained a victory over insolence. When David realized the true situation and heard for himself the challenge of Goliath the giant, he offered to respond and gained a victory over intimidation (1 Sam. 17:34-37). During the months that followed when Saul's jealousy devised various schemes to have David slain, he acted wisely (1 Sam. 18:14-15,30), and by so doing gained the victory over injustice. Eventually he had the opportunity of slaying Saul, and one of his chief men urged him to do so, but he refused to injure the Lord's anointed and preferred to wait God's time to be king of Israel (1 Sam. 24:3-16). This was a real victory over impatience.

In turning to the Saviour of the world we may recount that Christ subordinated aspirations through the waiting years and submitted to the Father's will, alone. He did not grow impatient as Moses did in Egypt and attempt His work of deliverance before the time. He succeeded triumphantly in counteracting the subtle suggestions of the tempter in the wilderness, alone. He supplicated in solitary vigil in an all night of prayer on the mount, and conquered, alone. He submerged personal aims and surpassed all former acts of yieldedness in accepting the cup of anguish in Gethsemane, alone. He suffered the excruciating agonies of the Cross and bore the shame and dishonor of sin, alone. He subjugated the greatest foe of the centuries, triumphing over the devil and death, alone. He secured unending dominion by ascending and being enthroned at the right hand of the Most High, alone. Of these seven victories of Christ there is no existing parallel in all history, since they outvie the record of David's conquests but corroborate His claim on the ground of moral majesty which confirms that He is the Offspring of David.

Let us advance yet another step. The greatest work by far achieved by David was his gathering together and unifying the twelve tribes under one scepter in a consolidated kingdom. In order to make this possible the Creator, Christ, caused David to grow up as the expression and exponent of the Spirit of Israel. In the natural sphere, Jacob was the progenitor of twelve sons and he named them after the twelve outstanding propensities of his own manifold character. The functions they fulfilled are indicated in the meanings attached to the twelve names bestowed, which names were divinely determined and destined to be engraven on the pearls that form the gates of the city of God. The twelve prominent privileges of spiritual life from sonship in Reuben the firstborn, through to heirship in Benjamin the youngest, are graphically illustrated.

In Jacob's history the twelvefold character he personified is divided into twelve separate personalities. In David's case the Lord reunites the twelve characteristics into one personality, therefore each tribe found its center in him. Then what do we discover in Christ as the Offspring of David? He came to gather together in one the people of God which are scattered abroad. But much more than this, He has made known the mystery of His will that in the dispensation of the fullness of times He will gather together in one all things in Christ both which are in earth and which are in Heaven even *in Him* (Eph. 1:9-10). He by whom every family in earth and Heaven is named, called twelve of the sons of Jacob and made them partakers of His divine nature. Dividing the foundation excellencies of His perfect character, He imprinted on Philip godlikeness, on Andrew goodness, on Peter graciousness, on John loving-kindness, through to the choice of Paul as one born out of due time, who bore the likeness of righteousness (note Phil. 3:9). The names of these twelve, in identification with the features of the divine nature, are engraved on the twelve foundation stones of the city of God.

We affirm afresh that Christ has fully and faithfully demonstrated in the Scriptures that He is the Offspring of David, in the forming of a spiritual family, in the fashioning of a social unity, in the framing of a celestial fraternity, and in the founding of an eternal monarchy wherein He shall reign forever and ever.

THE OVERCOMER

Be of good cheer; I have overcome the world (John 16:33).

To him that overcometh will I grant to sit with Me in My throne, even as I also overcame, and am set down with My Father in His throne (Rev. 3:21).

These shall make war with the Lamb, and the Lamb shall overcome them: for He is Lord of lords, and King of kings (Rev. 17:14).

During the whole period of the manifestation the courageous virtue and chivalrous valor of Christ were consistently visible in all His ministry. The same spirit has characterized His ministers, martyrs, and missionaries all down the ages. The secret of overcoming power, its strength and source are centered in the great Prevailer who has never been disheartened or discouraged and can never be defeated. He is always confident of bringing forth judgment unto victory (Isa. 42:3-4 RV). The Apostle Paul appears to have been contemplating this fact and was convinced of its reality when he wrote, "Thanks be unto God who always leadeth us in triumph in Christ, to make known the savour of His knowledge in every place" (2 Cor. 2:14 RV).

Christ has stood the severest tests of scrutiny and challenge through all the centuries and stands today as calm and composed as ever, undaunted, undismayed, and unafraid. As a mighty

Deliverer He cannot be displaced, as a majestic Defender He cannot be dislodged, and as the Dispenser of divine bounty He cannot be deposed.

Through the last decade of His waiting years in Nazareth, although zealously eager to enter upon His memorable ministry of helpfulness and healing, He never acted impatiently. Even Moses, the meekest of men, sought to deliver one of his brethren by slaying an Egyptian before he was called to emancipate his nation (Ex. 2:12).

When as Son of God Christ was tempted in the wilderness to express independence by exerting His creative right to make bread from stones, He declined forthright and quoted the Word of God as His bastion of defense in so doing. Thereupon the enemy sought to persuade Him to draw attention to His great importance, which is of such magnitude that angels had been charged to care for His person. "So then, why not do the sensational and spectacular thing and jump from the pinnacle of the three-storied temple, onto the pavement of the court in the midst of the crowd? Will not the appearing of angels deputed to protect Thee from harm impress the people of Your greatness and draw anthems of admiration and applause to Thyself?"

But Christ was not going to do a stunt to secure the bouquets of men, nor do an unnecessary miracle to see if God would fulfill His promise, which would have implied doubt. The third attempt was an appeal which was as good as asking Christ to be imperial and accept the scepter of world dominion which He could have for an act of homage. Christ again repaired to the Word of God for defense and completely foiled the foe. Be independent, be imposing, be imperial were the underlying strata of the subtle suggestions. The temptation in this physical realm was indicated by the symbols of bread, bouquets, and bribes, in the material realm it was associated with the wilderness, the land of promise, and the kingdom.

In the moral realm it pertained to a responsive obedience, observance, and obeisance, that is, obedience to the will of God, observance of the Word of God, and obeisance in the worship of God. In the intellectual realm the temptation was directed to the appeal of the body for its amenities, the aspiration of the soul for applause and admiration, and the ambition of the spirit for authority and administration. In the psychological realm the attempt to allure was made on the will, heart, and mind, which involved the whole personality volitionally, virtuously, and vocationally. These last three were identified with Christ's sonship, headship, and kingship. Other profound phases are included, but the mention of the triple attack in seven aspects gives us a little insight into the tremendous issues at stake, but our Lord's overcoming triumph was not confined solely to the wilderness temptation. When His public ministry was well-nigh completed, He told His disciples of the trials they could expect in the world, but added ample assurance to hearten them for meeting such tribulation by declaring, "Be of good cheer; I have overcome the world." This indicates that during the whole period of His ministry He encountered the opposition of the world. The term as it is used here constitutes the visible embodiment of a materialistic system with its maxims and manners that is obviously and obdurately opposed to the will and wisdom of God. In this organized constitution of things, carnal temperaments and tendencies dominate in the commercial, industrial, financial, cultural, musical, judicial, civil, and domestic circles. The nature of the mind of the mass of mankind is not subject to the law of God, neither indeed can be (Rom. 8:7).

Christ never pandered to this pretentious system at any time nor sought its patronage. On no occasion did He allow the acclamation and applaud of the crowd or the antagonism and accusations of the critics to sear His soul or seal His lips. He was entirely unmoved by the world's frown and unaffected by its friendly gestures. As Haldane wrote, "Alas for public impulse, the Lord is crucified, it clamoured for Barabbas and God's own son denied."

Never once did Christ modify the truth or minimize His warnings to suit the susceptibilities of His hearers, He pandered not to mortals high or low. He never misguided a soul or misdirected a life and was never guilty of maltreating or misleading anyone. With an irresistible charm and an impregnable fortitude He faced every accusation and allurement that wickedness could devise. In the potentiality of His inherent personal power He overcame the world and became the firstborn Son of consolation, and the foremost Champion of good cheer.

But what about this great world system of things that has continued its course since Christ ascended, and which is still opposed to His claims and control? Every leading nation has expressed its real nature by adopting as a national symbol a wild beast or wild bird. The brute-beast symbolism of the book of the Revelation of Christ signifies the amalgamated systems of government that are both faithless and ruthless, and which maintain a prayerless attitude toward Heaven and a pitiless attitude to humanity. Such organizations which are out to defy God, deify man, and disregard moral law are pictured marshaling their forces to make war with the Lamb (Rev. 17:12-14).

Christ is assailed in His sacrificial character as the Lamb, the character in which He gained His celebrated conquest over all the power of the enemy. Daniel was once called upon to face the ferocity and cruelty of wild beasts in a den of lions and received a demonstration to convince him that inferiority in physical power was far outmatched by superiority in spiritual prowess. His experience illustrates the nature of the conquest gained by the Son of man over dominating world empires. The lamblike character of His sacrificial submission does not savor of weakness, for the immediate statement declares He is Lord of Lords and King of kings (Rev. 17:14).

Christ never for one moment allowed Himself to be deflected from the main passion of His sacrificial life or from the master principle of submission to the will of God either by the devil, world dignitaries, or death itself.

THE ONLY-BEGOTTEN

We beheld His glory, the glory as of the only begotten of the
Father, full of grace and truth (John 1:14).

For God so loved the world, that He gave His only begotten
Son (John 3:16).

Begetment in deity is not to bring into existence but to give
expression, in comprehensible form, to that which already exists. Likewise, firstborn in the divine realm does not refer to a
beginning but to a manifestation, as for instance Christ is Firstborn from the dead, which constitutes a manifestation of His
mastery over the power of death. Or again, Firstborn of all
creation, which sets forth the manifestation of His priority to all
things visible.

Embedded in this begetment lies the eternal, essential, and
effectual reality of oneness to which Christ referred in His perfect priestly prayer (John 17:21). The Only-begotten is therefore
the first and final expression in all fullness of the Father, so that
in oneness of will and purpose deity is agreeably, amicably, and
abidingly a unique unity, in unanimity and absolute harmony.

The only-begotten Son is the eternal fountain of essential
fullness, from whom emanates the ever-flowing freshness of
grace and truth. In His full-orbed beauty, Christ combines in
perfect oneness the matchless attributes of deity, blends the
multiform variegations of light, voices the mystical vibrations of
infinite love, and verifies the manifold virtues of life everlasting.
Therefore, the Only-begotten Son is the manifest expression of
the Father in the faithfulness of His loving-kindness, in the
perfectness of His living likeness, and in the preciousness of His
transparent truthfulness.

In other words, Christ is the visible manifestation in perfect
manhood of the invisible godhead. He unites and binds in one
personality a beautiful countenance, a boundless compassion,
and a beneficent covenant. Little wonder that from the first
chapter of John's message to the last, He is set forth as the one
center of attraction for witnesses and the object of heart adora-

tion for worshipers. Moses pitched the tent in which God dwelt in the midst of the tents of Israel, but by virtue of the Word becoming flesh, Christ pitched the tent in which the Father dwells in the midst of mankind. God no longer confines His earthly sanctuary of abode to one people, but as the prophet stated, "The God of the whole earth shall He be called" (Isa. 54:5). Let us not lose sight of this precious fact that He who is the Only-begotten Son and is the full and final expression of the Father's glory, is the same that becomes the love gift that is given to humanity in John 3:16: "For God so loved the world, that He gave His only begotten Son." The giving of the Only-begotten for a perishing world is love's greatest gift.

By virtue of the super-excellence of the Son, who is preeminently superior in His distinctive moral perfections and who personally possesses spiritual riches in glory that are of inestimable value, we learn that He not only answers adequately for the enormous debt of sin, but erases the awful record of evil deeds by destroying their existence. There is therefore now no remaining trace of evidence by which a reconciled soul can be accused of sin or condemned. This constitutes the precious truth of justification. The degree of vindication that divine justice has received far outweighs the dishonor that has been incurred. The splendor of the august merit of Christ on the one hand overwhelms and obliterates the awful squalor of human guilt on the other. "Behold the Lamb of God, which taketh away the sin of the world" (John 1:29).

In His transparent character as the truth, the Only-begotten prevails over all that is tainted with corruption and error and remains untarnished in His transcendent triumph (see Zeph. 3:5). The Son soars loftily above and beyond the sordid heights of sin and abides unrivaled in the glorious grandeur of infinite grace, for where sin abounded, grace did much more than superabound.

By this inestimable earnest of the inheritance of the saints in light, God has lavished His most precious treasure on those least deserving, and how will He not also with Him freely give us all things? Verily the cross of Christ has been made by God to become the key of spiritual knowledge, the door of celestial wisdom, the crown of impartial justice, the scepter of eternal mercy, the center of perennial righteousness, the sign of vital reconciliation, the heart of supernal love, and the diadem of immortal glory.

> What will He not bestow
> Who freely gave this mighty gift unbought,
> Unmerited, unheeded, and unsought,
> What will He not bestow!

The Son is the only one who fully resembles the Father's features, fitly represents the Father's fullness, and finally reveals the Father's faithfulness. No one knows the Father save the Son. Therefore He described to the woman at Jacob's well the true character of spiritual worship and was able, because of His perfect knowledge, to assure her that the Father sought and cherished such worship from the spiritually minded.

Christ in the comeliness of His character as the Only-begotten Son, is the crown of the covenant of compassion which Heaven confirmed. He it is who magnifies the mercy of the majestic mediation that has been provided. He Himself beautifies the beneficence of the blessings bestowed. He by His spotless sacrifice stabilizes the security of salvation and soul satisfaction eternally.

THE OMNIPOTENT ONE

Ah, Lord God! behold, Thou hast made the heaven and the earth by Thy great power and stretched out arm, and there is nothing too hard for Thee (Jer. 32:17).

Alleluia: for the Lord God omnipotent reigneth. Let us be glad and rejoice, and give honour to Him (Rev. 19:6-7).

Echoing down the centuries from the messages of the prophets, from the mandate of the Law, and ofttimes repeated in the manifold meditations of the psalms, we hear one predominant note, reverberating loudly and resounding clearly, which proclaims to the world and all its generations the overruling majesty of godhead.

The fact is eventually crystalized into one brief declaration, "The Lord God omnipotent reigneth." Hudson Taylor, in China, uttered these words when the news first reached him of the Boxer uprising and the beheading of missionaries.

Little consideration is given in Scripture to the fancied rights and fictitious claims made by man, but rather an attitude of wonder and worship is frequently expressed, that the Almighty should regard man at all, and the infinite Creator be mindful of him (Ps. 8:4; 144:3).

During His earthly manifestation our Lord and Saviour displayed and declared that He held every prerogative of supreme sovereignty. The reality of this He demonstrated by the munificence of His mercy in sympathizing with the afflicted, by the maintenance of His ministry in seeking and saving the lost, and by the magnificence of His majesty, in subduing all the powers of evil and in subjugating the devil.

No other champion ever undertook to do on man's behalf so much for so many, singlehanded. Christ holds the unique and solitary rank of being the only Canceller and Justifier in relation to sin, the sole Comforter in sorrow who binds up the broken in heart, the only Conferrer of life and immortality, and the first and final Conqueror of death. How amazing it is to contemplate that when in meekness He harnessed His might to minister to mankind and allowed Himself to be despised, yet in His almightiness He despiseth not any (Job 36:5). Yea, and a broken and contrite heart He will not despise (Ps. 51:17), and not even the prayer of the destitute goes unheeded (Ps. 102:17).

What stately qualifications belong to Christ, for He holds in rightful possession such an adequacy of potential power, that He is abundantly able to do anything, anywhere, for anyone, at any time, that is in any wise necessary.

We speak of this as His omnipotence, but how poorly the reality is conveyed to the mind by the use of such a word.

When we say the stars are enormous, it does not describe the beauty of their brilliance. To state that the sky is spacious fails to convey the vastness of its magnitude. If we speak of the sun as voluminous, the statement falls far short of depicting its energy, sovereignty, and therapy. To announce that the equinoxes are marvelous does not adequately tell of their regularity and unvariableness in influencing the seasons year by year. To intimate that the upholding of the universe is miraculous only partially suggests that infinite power wielded by the authoritative word of the Creator, Christ. Therefore, if we proclaim that His name is glorious, the term is far too restricted in its range of meaning to even casually impart a circumscribed idea of the superior excellence and surpassing luster of His eternal magnificence.

According to the calculations of science, three billion six hundred and fifty million tons of matter are broken up every quarter of an hour for supplying the inconceivable amount of atomic power necessary for maintaining this universal system. We realize incalculable measures are necessary to generate the power for furnishing light and heat that must traverse a distance of over ninety-two million miles to furnish the specific requirements for this earth alone. This prodigious source of maintenance has continued through the centuries without any apparent diminution of supplies. No wonder we find written in Scripture the divine question, "Behold, I am the Lord, the God of all flesh: is there anything too hard for me?" (Jer. 32:27)

In the light of the divine omnipotence, those who mourn their loss in bereavement have this supreme reason for submitting to the divine will, and all who are grievously afflicted should find in this truth their chief factor for consolation, "The Lord God omnipotent reigneth."

The patriarch Job refused to attribute his losses to the Sabeans or to any secondary cause, but stated confidently, "The Lord hath given, the Lord hath taken away, blessed be the name of the Lord."

In the truceless warfare of this transient life, we need to be constantly furnished with strength to sustain, supplies to maintain, and sufficient sympathy to hearten, together with the absolute assurance of ultimate victory, all of which and much more is guaranteed in the Saviour omnipotent. This truth is too often treated without its mature historical setting, without the magnitude of its universal scope, without the magnificence of its moral strength, and without the sure maintenance of its eternal sovereignty. As a detail of its many facets that may be practically availed of in everyday life, Christ taught, "whatsoever ye shall ask in My name, that will I do, that the Father may be glorified in the Son" (John 14:13).

> Is prayer a force or just a farce?
> The way He brings His will to pass
> Assures to faith how very real
> Is God's reply to man's appeal.
>
> He sees, He knows, He loves, He cares,
> He hears the pleadings of our prayers,
> And plans His blessings in disguise,
> To give the soul a glad surprise.
>
> He sure delights to test our trust,
> He does not wish to see it rust,
> So wings an answer from the skies,
> That all our fancied hope outvies.
>
> C.J.R.

How radiantly we should rejoice in the knowledge that the omnipotent Lord Himself is the stronghold of wisdom and might, the citadel of truth and light, the center of peace and rest, the fountain of love and mercy, yea, and the celestial castle of every other imperishable attribute that is attributable to deity. Each and all of these incorruptible realities are blended most beautifully in His perfect character. Together they express the glory of holiness in one harmonious whole. Possessed of these infinite capacities of competence, Messiah not only assures the fulfillment of the divine purpose but confirms to the redeemed His absolute ability as Saviour to secure a complete propitation, a fully furnished provision, and an inviolate perfection forever. Such a Christ is able to save, able to secure, able to sustain, and able to satisfy the perfected capacities of His people eternally.

THE OMNISCIENT ONE

Lord, Thou knowest all things (John 21:17).
Neither is there any creature that is not manifest in His sight: but all things are naked and open unto the eyes of Him with whom we have to do (Heb. 4:13).
He knew all men, and needed not that any should testify of man (John 2:24-25).
I am God, and there is none else. . . . Declaring the end from the beginning (Isa. 46:9-10).

The foresight, insight, and oversight in relation to world affairs belong solely to an omniscient Christ. These matters relate to the foresight of His providence, the insight of His governance, and the oversight of His prescience. These capacities supply credentials that adequately qualify Him to administer His purpose universally. The Apostle John is careful to tell us that our precious Saviour in His manifestation knew all men, and needed not that any should testify of man: for He knew what was in man (John 2:25).

Wherefore Christ never needed an introduction to anyone, nor did He require a description of any personal character or any information whatsoever as to one's whereabouts. He knew inherently every name, nature, and nationality on the face of the earth. He knew immediately without needing to be told. His knowledge was all-inclusive and therefore infinite, no matter if the individual be of the Roman, Grecian, or Hebrew nation, or linked with the Scythian, Caucasion, or Mongolian race. He knew the habits and habitations of all, their countries and customs, their language and labor, and their hearts and hopes.

John immediately demonstrates these facts by describing seven characters with whom Christ had personal dealings. Nicodemus, although a man of noble birth, was disqualified for the kingdom of Heaven. The wanton woman of Samaria was dissatisfied in spite of all her indulgence. The man at the pool of Bethseda was disabled regardless of God's regular providential dealings. The nobleman's son was diseased although his father was in a position to summon the best medical skill. The woman accused in the temple courts was defiled although every means of cleansing through ceremonial offerings, ministering priests, and altars was adjacent and available. The man born blind was in darkness while environed with solar and lunar light, yea, ethical, moral, and spiritual light. Lazarus was dead in the face of all forms of provision being accessible to sustain life.

These seven characters present a complete view of the desperate need of mankind and demonstrate the necessity for a new moral birth which could be brought about only through the operation of the spirit of God. Christ knew the existing state of things and said to the most cultured of the seven, "That which is born of the flesh is flesh. . . . Marvel not that I said unto thee, Ye must be born again" (John 3:6-7).

By exercising His regenerative power He gave to Nicodemus suitability to enter the kingdom. By expressing His resourceful power He implanted satisfaction in the heart of the woman of Samaria by creating within her a springing well of life. By virtue of His ransoming power He reclaimed and restored the nobleman's son to soundness of health. By exerting His resolute power He imparted ability to the impotent man. By expressing His redemptive power toward the woman in the temple court He secured to her a sanctity which delivered her from condemnation. He expressed to the man born blind His revealing power and gave him the sight that sees and knows. He exercised His resurrection power in the case of Lazarus, who was already corrupting in the sepulcher, and gave him social status that commended widespread investigation and inquiry so that all Jerusalem went out to see him. This sevenfold demonstration prepares us to listen later to the greater claim He made in those universally known words, "All power is given unto Me in heaven and on earth." In His omniscience He knew perfectly well what mankind needed most, and He knew full well He was able to supply that need.

The entire record of John in this regard is most revealing. The Lord clearly comprehended the real significance of what He was doing when He gave a summons to Abraham to take his only son whom he loved and offer him in sacrifice on a hill that would be shown to him. The Lord Himself promoted the journey to Mount Moriah and prompted Abraham to say, "My son, God will provide Himself a lamb." Not, "God will provide a lamb Himself," but "He Himself is the lamb provided." Centuries later the realization was impressed on John, the herald, who said as he saw Jesus approaching at Jordan, "Behold the Lamb of God" (John 1:29). The same Lord was fully aware, when He commanded Moses in the wilderness to make a serpent of brass and erect it on a pole, what that brazen serpent was to signify, which He stated in John 3:14. As the omniscient one He constrained Jacob to give the parcel of land by the well of Sychar to his son Joseph as a precursor to symbolize the priceless gift He would bestow in the well of life. Yea, He ordained and overruled all the significant features of Israel's history with a definite foresight and determined objective.

How obvious this matter becomes when we consider the local settings of His memorable ministry—the timely arrival outside the city of Nain when the funeral of the only son of a widow emerged (Luke 7:12), the appropriate moment He chose to approach the storm-tossed disciples on Galilee (Matt. 14:25), the delayed advance toward Bethany to allow for the burial of Lazarus in the sepulcher in preparation for a display of His resurrecting power. He appeared in every case at the opportune time as a testimony to the truth of His omniscience.

> Say not my soul from whence shall God relieve thy care?
> Remember that omniscience hath servants everywhere.
> His methods are sublime, His heart profoundly kind,
> God never is before His time, and never is behind.

With a clear consciousness of all commencements as well as consummations, He was never taken by surprise or startled by anyone, and never mastered by circumstances.

He foretold in detail the conditions that would characterize the destruction of Jerusalem and described the final universal doom. Christ knew Abraham was living and had the knowledge that Moses, whom he predeceased by four hundred years, had written books (Luke 16:29). He knew that marriage did not pertain among angels, but that they rejoiced when sinners repented (Matt. 22:30; Luke 15:10). He knew that the names of the disciples were written in Heaven (Luke 10:20). He knew the hour would come when all that were in the graves would hear His voice and come forth (John 5:28).

When Jacob made his great forecast of the future of Israel, he told his sons that in the last days Zebulun would be a harbor for ships (Gen. 49:13). Three thousand years elapsed ere the coast of Palestine was surveyed by marine engineers, and although petitions containing over sixty thousand names were submitted, asking for the harbor to be built opposite Tel Aviv, the construction was carried out in Zebulun's former territory at Haifa. The mind that moved Jacob to speak, that directed the prophets of Israel to declare their predictions, and that enlightened Daniel to describe the development of world kingdoms, is perfect in perception, complete in comprehension, absolute in apprehension, and infinite in intelligence. There is no searching of His understanding, He knows everything about everyone everywhere and has told us the end from the beginning (Isa. 46:10). He is Omniscient.

THE OMNIPRESENT ONE

Whither shall I go from Thy spirit? or whither shall I flee from Thy presence? If I ascend up into heaven, Thou art there. . . . If I take the wings of the morning, and dwell in the uttermost parts of the sea; Even there shall Thy hand lead me, and Thy right hand shall hold me. . . . Yea, the darkness hideth not from Thee; but the night shineth as the day: the darkness and the light are both alike to Thee (Ps. 139:7-10,12).

"Even there" (Ps. 139:10), "Even so" (Matt. 11:26), "Even now" (John 11:22), are expressions which intimate His omnipresence, omniscience, and omnipotence, as their contexts prove. These three words are used in the Latin version of the Bible, omnipotent being the only one that appears in our English translation.

The all-pervading presence of the Eternal One stands out conspicuously among the choicest realities of divine revelation and is in the forefront of all Christian experience. The assurance and realization of this inestimable blessing become inexpressibly precious in the path of life to every believing soul. The Highest Himself has greatly honored humanity by manifestly appearing and faithfully assuring us of His abiding presence, not only by demonstration but also by declaration in those memorable words, "Lo, I am with you alway, even unto the end of the age."

The thrill of a real Lover's nearness may therefore become an everyday experience. The truth that this great Leader and Guide, the Captain of our salvation, is close by in every conflict both heartens the soul with sheer enjoyment and furnishes the life with fresh courage, to fight the good fight of faith with a firmer resolve. The ever-present One is never missing in the hour of trial, whether it be in the burning fiery furnace with His children (Dan. 3:25), in the billowing storm with His commissioned disciples (Matt. 8:26), in the benighted valley of the shadow with His chosen companions (Ps. 23:4), or in the banishment of Patmos with John His close friend (Rev. 1:9-10). His wonderful pledge, "I will never, no never, leave thee," is colorful with fragrant consolation, cheerful with fervent consideration, and Christful with final compensation. His ever-abiding presence is the true source of ceaseless enlightenment (John 8:12), the real secret of endless enjoyment (Ps. 16:11), and the sacred sphere of boundless enlargement (Ps. 4:1).

If we have never known the delight of an intimate friendship in our earthly associations, it is not likely that we would feel isolation too keenly. Much more is this true in spiritual relationships. If we have never enjoyed the intimacy of His nearness we do not feel distance. What has been called "the practice of the presence of God" opens avenues of abounding pleasure in communion and we learn to comprehend more of the attractive perfections of our precious Saviour and the unutterable glories of His personal character. His presence may be realized in a variety of vocations in which He functions in order to fulfill the purposes of grace.

By virtue of His manifestation in manhood in order to substantiate His right to redeem, His mediation in priesthood to negotiate the will of the covenant, and His ministration in shepherdhood to facilitate the disbursement of facilities for the flock of God, we recognize the matchless values of His Saviourhood and visualize at once the desirability of His friendship and fellowship. Where else may we find another presence that provides such profound moral privileges and furnishes such renowned spiritual blessings as those suggested by His filling these official capacities?

The Gospel of John is a veritable storehouse of sublimities that supplies us with a graphic portrayal of what the divine presence means the world over to all mankind. For instance, what would be the significance of the Lamb of God, the ladder of Jacob, the love-gift of God, the living water, the living bread, the light of the world, the life in resurrection, and the love of the Father without Him? Although throughout John's message precious sayings are filtering from the Saviour's gracious lips, we also find perfect love flowing from His generous heart.

The predominant lesson we learn in the light of His countenance is linked with the intensity and immensity of His own personal love, which constitutes the largest legacy of His everlasting presence.

The very environment of that presence which was assured to Moses of old (Ex. 33:14), and which saved Israel (Isa. 63:9), is now become the experience of the disciples to enlighten and enlarge their spiritual comprehension. In the atmosphere of that sacred presence they learn that Christ loves *intimately*. They repeatedly hear Him use the personal pronouns, "as I have loved you ... continue ye in My love." He came from the invisible realm into the visible to verify and demonstrate divine love. His works confirmed His words, His deeds substantiated His sayings. We do not infer that He loves intimately, He Himself intimated it. Later John writes, "Hereby we perceive love, because He laid down His life for us." Such love is richest in bounty, fairest in fidelity, strongest in sympathy, choicest in constancy, sweetest in sincerity, mightiest in majesty, and greatest in glory.

In His presence we are assured that He loves *intensely*. Having loved His own which were in the world He loved them unto the uttermost, and no less. In the entire universe there is but one parallel and one only to the depth and degree of His love. This is not found in earthly relationships whatever they be. The affectionate love of Boaz for Ruth, the admirable love of Jonathan for David in no sense signify the true character of Christ's love to us. The only parallel that exists is in the magnificent and munificent quality of the Father's love for the Son. "*As my* Father hath loved Me, *so* have I loved you." Can we have a shadow of doubt about the Father's love for His beloved Son? Can we define its depth? Can we describe its strength? Can we declare its magnitude? So boundless, shoreless, ageless, such is His love for us.

In His presence we are assured that He loves *immutably*. His love is unchanging in faithfulness, unvarying in freshness, unabating in fullness, and undying in friendliness. Never for a moment can there be the slightest sensation of subsidence in the high tide of love's honor and holiness. Never for a split second can there be the faintest degree of decline in the full-orbed glow of love's fervor and fidelity. Never for an atom of space can there be the smallest shadow of eclipse across the sunlike face of love's devotion and durability. Anything that is immutable in character never develops or diminishes, never enlarges or contracts, and never varies or vanishes. Nothing can stem or stifle, quell or quench the vast volume of His virtuous and vivacious love. "The Son of God who loved me and gave Himself for me."

In His presence we are assured that He loves *infinitely*. His Lordly mien, as Lord of lords, His lovely meed as King of kings, and His lofty mace as God of gods, signify undetermined capacities, undefined faculties, and underived attributes. The One who is highest in greatness and holiest in glory and who eternally expresses the immortal excellences and perfections of the god-head, loves infinitely, in the almightiness of His everlasting strength. If we could scale the highest altitude, or stand in the deepest depth, or scan the remotest star, such dimensions as we might discover would be dwarfed into insignificance in the light and sight of His heavenly love and likeness. When we enter into His presence in the moral suitability required for access which His love supplies, and lean the head on His bosom as John did, eyes become clearer, ears become keener, joy becomes deeper, rest becomes sweeter, hearts become warmer, peace becomes greater, and hope becomes brighter than ever before to the Christian who really believes.

> Christ is not so far away as to be even near,
> He's near of Kin,
> Our bodies are the temples He holds most dear,
> He dwells within.

THE OFFERER

For Christ is not entered into the holy places made with hands . . . nor yet that He should offer Himself often. . . . For then must He often have suffered . . . once in the end of the age hath He appeared to put away sin by the sacrifice of Himself. . . . So Christ was once offered to bear the sins of many (Heb. 9:24-26,28).
After He had offered one sacrifice for sins (Heb. 10:12).

The elaborate system of sacrifice associated with Old Testament ritual made no provision for the offerer to enter the sanctuary where God's presence dwelt, nor did the high priest of Israel, who was officially appointed to enter the holiest once a year, have the right or hold the privilege to remain there. The sanctuary under the Mosaic system was a sphere of specified service, not a habitation of rest where the official could remain in residence. The animal sacrifices offered by the Aaronic priest-hood, even though they were presented regularly and reverent-ly, were ineffectual and could never prove to be an actual substitute for man. The value of these offerings lay in what they signified in symbol and portrayed in principle.

The character of the covenant then existing demanded a continual repetition, a constant bringing of similar sacrifices which never gave the offerer real rest of soul or perfect peace of mind. Therefore the entire Aaronic system has been super-seded, and at once pales before the radiant presence of One whose superior nature and stately office qualify Him to trans-place that which is imperfect.

Christ offered the greatest offering that was ever made. No such sacrifice was ever known throughout the universe. He offered Himself through the eternal Spirit without spot to God. By virtue of His vicarious death and victorious resurrection He ascended and entered the celestial sanctuary and sat down on the right hand of God. His sitting down signifies that He took possession of the sacred realm where God is throned in majesty. (Today when workers decide on a sit-down strike, they take full possession of the premises.) Our Blessed Lord in His official capacity as High Priest is Son over the house of God and resides there forevermore. Accordingly we are told that He entered as the Forerunner for us, which assurance furnishes the guarantee that we also shall follow and be dwellers in the house of the Lord forever. For this very reason He is able to save to the uttermost because He ever liveth to make intercession for us.

The efficiency and efficacy of His precious offering not only enable Him to enter the holiest, but entitle Him to remain there as a righteous and replete Redeemer, representing His people. All power is His to rule, ransom, regenerate, and reconcile, yea, all the resourceful power of administration. He remains in resi-dence where no one else had the right to stay in order to distribute royal bounties and rich bequests, and to dispense regal blessings through angelic agencies, which are sent forth to minister to the heirs of salvation. Our minds are incapable of grasping the momentous issues resulting, for God's name has been glorified, His law magnified, His claims gratified, His rights satisfied, and His justice justified.

The acceptability of Christ's offering can never be increased, the values of His reconciling grace cannot be improved, and the fullness of blessing secured can never be implemented by any-one anywhere.

A distinctive sufficiency and exclusive sublimity mark the offering Christ made of Himself, which exceeds in value all other oblations. The fact that He sat down, which is stressed five times by use of the words "sit," "sat," and "set," in the Hebrew message, means nothing less than eternal merit. On this basis we are assured of unending maintenance through the unvarying mediation of an unchanging Messiah. He perfects forever them that are sanctified. As sons and daughters of the living God every member of the household is made suitable in character and nature to a degree of sanctity which benefits the celestial sanctuary of the Most High.

When Christ entered for us, He took the noblest post of highest honor in those nameless heights of perpetual glory that He might fill all things. Greater evidence than this to assure that the everlasting covenant has been confirmed could not be given. Fuller assurance that the final contract has been completed could not possibly be produced. Richer guarantees of continual acceptance other than those we already have could never be drafted. We are given unqualified rights as fellow citizens with the saints and of the household of God and are destined to be received into the Father's house as our home eternal which is pervaded by love and beautified with the glowing effulgence of the everlasting light of the Lamb. Even now we have an earnest in the holy privilege of boldly entering into the holiest by the blood of Jesus. We may enter because He is already there. He affirmed to Nathanael that he would see Heaven open, and He opened it.

The offering of Himself was verily the key,
  By which our Sovereign Lord
Unlocked the door of immortality to you and me,
  And entering in Himself before, He set it wide forevermore,
That we by His love sanctified, and by His free grace justified,
  Might enter in all fearlessly and dwell forever by His side.

John Oxenham

THE ONLY WISE GOD

Now unto the King eternal, immortal, invisible, the only wise God, be honour and glory for ever and ever. Amen (1 Tim. 1:7).

In the Scripture this is rendered the "only God," which is in keeping with the frequently repeated statement of the prophet Isaiah, "There is no God else beside Me. . . . Look unto Me, and be ye saved, all the ends of the earth: for I am God, and there is none else. . . . That they may know from the rising of the sun, and from the west, that there is none beside Me. I am the Lord, and there is none else" (Isa. 45:21-22,6). The Apostle Paul likewise confirms these declarations by saying there is none other God but one. "For though there be that are called gods, whether in heaven or in earth, [as there be gods many, and lords many,] But to us there is but one God, the Father, of whom are all things, and we in Him; and one Lord Jesus Christ, by whom are all things, and we by Him" (1 Cor. 8:5-6).

Here again we alight upon the inconceivable, the incomprehensible, and the incomparable, concerning which eye hath not seen nor ear heard, neither have entered into the heart of man to conceive (1 Cor. 2:9). How is it possible for us in our thinking to go back to a state before the world was, prior to scintillating stars or shining sun, before the seas and seasons existed—a condition ere creation was wrought, ere cherubim flew, or the cerulean arch appeared in the heights—back before angelic hosts thronged the celestial courts, or comets had orbits, or winds their circuits? In the vestibule of a calm and holy sanctity the eternal One with supreme sovereignty abode alone, awesome in immaculate purity, absolute in immutable authority, and almighty in immortal majesty. Resting in the serenity of perfect grandeur, the immaculate Mind in solitary sufficiency determined the eternal purpose.

Well might the prophet ask, "With whom took He counsel?" or the greatest of apostles exclaim, "O the depth of the riches both of the wisdom and knowledge of God, how unsearchable are His judgments and His ways past finding out." Even wisdom's seven pillars were not as yet hewn (Prov. 9:1), when the strongest, stateliest, sublimest will contemplated and concluded a determinate decision to create and bring innumerable worlds into being. The bosom of eternity was then born, the indestructible Word expressed, the counsels of His omnipotent will recorded, and the exhibition of His wondrous works disclosed. Minds were created for comprehension, eyes were made for perception, nerves were formed for sensation, wills were framed for decision, hearts were molded for affection, and a myriad of other marvels were created which have increased in their importance and influence throughout the centuries.

We may attribute the advance in the values of these capacities to the benefits of intuition, inspiration, investigation, and invention, all of which features develop the intellectual faculties, enabling the mind to comprehend more fully the works of the Creator and the wonders of creation. If we have difficulty in believing that the infinite Creator and only wise God communicates with His creature man, we need but consider the questionnaire given to Job, which is recorded in the closing chapters of the book which bears his name.

Twelve of the questions that are asked deal with marvels of the inanimate realm and refer to light and lightning, the earth and the heavens, the sea and the snow. Light does not dwell in some huge abysmal well, but in a "way," and is constantly traveling at a prodigious speed, hence the scientific accuracy of the question asked in Job 38:19. Even the electromagnetic waves which carry the voice around the entire globe in a matter of seconds are the subject of the question in Job 38:35. The only wise God is familiar with every last feature of His creation.

Following the inanimate, there are twelve questions which concern animate things. These wonders conclude with an interrogation relative to the origin of the tenacious strength of the lion, the telescopic eye of the eagle, and the tremendous speed of the hawk. More ponderously profound are the questions concerning Mazzoreth, which is the Hebrew word for the Zodiac, a diagram of the heavens divided into twelve sections marking the main stars visible between a belt of from sixteen to eighteen degrees during each month of the year. The mention of Pleiades and its influence is of immense interest. This constellation which governs the revolutions of the sun is estimated as being thousands of billions of miles away and its controlling power was originated and is maintained by the only wise God our Saviour. The terms used in Scripture are accommodated to human capacity, hence Job is asked if he can bind the sweet influences of Pleiades or unloose the bands that bind the powers of Orion. If the Lord were to express cosmic data in terms of exact science the profoundest human mind would not understand a single statement. Man has neither the wisdom to construct nor the will power to control spheres of such dimensions and distances of such degrees.

Yet, the greatest display by far of the unerring wisdom of God is to be traced in the realm of the moral activities of deity. The incessant working on unparralleled designs of unending deliverance for man, under the unceasing dominance of the Most High, betokens the fact that an eternal purpose has been definitely determined which no enemy, however formidable, is able to foil or frustrate.

Therefore, when the apostle makes this statement and speaks of the only wise God, we possess in the scope of revealed truth the spacious background of established evidence which, when consulted, not only fully warrants the wording of the declaration but overwhelmingly confirms and substantiates the same. Wisdom's wisest works are not exhausted in the wonders of creation but are reserved for and witnessed in the perfect work of redemption, and in exercising the prerogative of regeneration.

Wisdom's most marvelous sign to a ruined race is startling in the extreme. "Behold, a virgin shall conceive, and bear a son, and shall call His name Immanuel" (Isa. 7:14).

Wisdom's best bestowment is intensely consoling, "For unto us a child is born, unto us a Son is given: and the government shall be upon His shoulder: and His name shall be called Wonderful Counsellor, The mighty God, The everlasting Father, The Prince of Peace. Of the increase of His government and peace there shall be no end" (Isa. 9:6-7).

Wisdom's finest favor is bestowed upon us through the First-born, "But of Him are ye in Christ Jesus, who of God is made unto us wisdom, and righteousness, and sanctification, and redemption" (1 Cor. 1:30).

Wisdom's purest pleasure is the establishment of permanent peace in an environment of perpetual joy (Ps. 16:11).

Wisdom's largest legacy is bequeathed in the Lord of glory whose amaranthine love in its breadth, length, depth, and height surpasseth knowledge (Eph. 3:18-19).

Wisdom's greatest glory is the grace of God and the gift by grace which is by one man Jesus Christ (Rom. 5:15).

Wisdom's stateliest sympathy is expressed in the Father's sending of His Son to be the Saviour of the world (1 John 4:14).

Wisdom's clearest call is heralded by the Saviour's invitation, "Come unto Me, all ye that labour and are heavy laden, and I will give you rest. . . . Him that cometh to Me I will in no wise cast out" (Matt. 11:28; John 6:37).

Wisdom's sweetest song is voiced by a redeemed host who join in the immortal refrain, "Thou art worthy . . . for Thou wast slain, and hast redeemed us to God by Thy blood out of every kindred, and tongue, and people, and nation; And hast made us unto our God kings and priests" (Rev. 5: 9-10).

Wisdom's choicest conferment consists of the crowns by which Christ has been coronated in view of His many celebrated conquests, "on His head were many diadems" (Rev 19:12).

Wisdom's comeliest Captain is the chiefest among ten thou-sand and the altogether lovely (S. of Sol. 5:16).

Wisdom's divinest deliverance includes the defeat of the devil and the destruction of death (Heb. 2:14; 1 Cor. 15: 26,54).

The radiant record of wisdom's worthiest work is confined solely to the Scriptures of truth. None of the philosophies, theos-ophies, and sophistries of men in existence among nations, contains anything comparable to the immutable wisdom of the infinite God. That the world by its system of wisdom knew not God is a fact emphasized by the Holy Spirit at the very citadel and center of Grecian philosophy. Alongside this startling state-ment, we meet the Heaven-hewn affirmation, "Christ the power of God, and the wisdom of God" (1 Cor. 1:24).

> Teach me but Christ, all wisdom you bestow.
> Teach me all else, I less than nothing know.

THE OWL OF THE DESERT

I am like an owl of the desert (Ps. 102:6).

This striking similitude is one of seven that is made relative to Christ in the Scriptures involving and invading the realm of ornithology, a science which pays its tribute in aiding us to apprehend the manifold nature of the activities wrought by the Redeemer. Of the seven birds mentioned, every one possesses a specific characteristic that is exemplified by the Saviour in carrying out His wonderful work of redemption for mankind. We are all aware that the eagle expresses superiority, the hen sympathy, the pigeon sacrifice, the dove sorrow, the pelican solitude, the owl separation, and the sparrow substitution. Some-thing of the mysterious is always attached to divine selection, equally as much as in divine election.

When choosing the seven figures of service from the features of bird life the Creator was well aware of their distinctive traits and instinctive habits. He furnished the lofty superiority signified in the eagle, the lonely solitude suggested in the pelican, the

lovely sympathy symbolized in the hen, and the lowly submission set forth in the sparrow. Each of these characteristic features is displayed in the ministry of Christ to an inimitable
degree during His sacrificial work, by means of which He secured eternal redemption. We should greatly prize these pictures of the Saviour's precious perfections, displayed in His
demeanor and disclosed in His behavior during the whole period of His labor of love.

In the superiority displayed by the eagle over external surroundings and in the air-supremacy it demonstrates, there is
given a clear witness to its competent strength. The ability which
enables this bird to soar above the stateliest pinnacles of towering mountain peaks, its efficient mastery of atmospheric conditions in combating tempestuous winds, its intrepid speed, and
wonderful powers of respiration in rarefied air, its resis-
tance to extreme temperatures of cold or heat, its apparent
tireless exertion in carrying live food to its young at enormous
heights, its unparalleled vision in being able to see small creatures when miles distant, combine to establish an all-around
superiority toward every phase of its physical surroundings.

From the seven instances in the Old Testament in which
analogies are drawn connecting features of this denizen of the
air to the actions of deity, we select but one for brevity's sake.
"*As* the eagle stirreth up her nest, fluttereth over her young with
her wings: *so* the Lord alone did lead them" (Deut. 32:11). What
a graphic picture this is of the sustaining strength of the divine
might in its benevolent sufficiency. The eagle-faced cherub of
the four cherubim depicted in the prophecy of Ezekiel and
confirmed by John's vision on Patmos, was applied by the early
fathers to the character of the content of John's Gospel. Therein
the superiority of Christ in the mystery of His deity is portrayed,
overcoming all physical diseases, material difficulties, and de-
moniacal powers. Christ rose prevailingly above all obstacles
that confronted His mission of mercy, no matter what form they
took, in obdurately and obstinately opposing His authority. He
lived and labored above the barriers of national, racial, legal,

and traditional prejudices, and never permitted the superstitions that were current to curb or curtail His compassion for the needy and His care for the heavy-laden.

What a captivating picture of attentive regard and affectionate interest is to be seen when a brood of young chicks nestles beneath the wings of the mother hen. Our Lord laid hold of this attractive figure when as King of grief He wept in anguish of soul over favored Jerusalem and gave utterance to those memorable words, "O Jerusalem, Jerusalem, thou that killest the prophets, and stonest them which are sent unto thee, how often would I have gathered thy children together, even as a hen gathereth her chickens under her wings, and ye would not!" (Matt. 23:37)

How expressive is this of the tenderness of Christ's character, the gentleness of His care, and the kindliness of His compassion! No metaphor could more clearly express the amiableness of His attitude toward His people who rejected His ministry and repelled His mercy.

Quite a number of the psalms are graced with the beauty of the feature of paternity in godhead. What recollections are woven about the warmth of welcome received, and the wonderful refuge afforded beneath God's sheltering wings! David desired the divine defense when he said, "Shew me Thy marvellous lovingkindness . . . Keep me as the apple of Thine eye, hide me under the shadow of Thy wings" (Ps. 17:7-8). When on another occasion he declared his personal decision he stated, "I will abide in Thy tabernacle for ever: I will trust in the covert of Thy wings" (Ps. 61:4). God had illustrated His attitude in the Tabernacle wherein two cherubim with extended wings stood above the mercy seat.

David likewise realized his supreme delight in the same sanctuary, "Because Thou hast been my help, therefore in the shadow of Thy wings will I rejoice" (Ps. 63:7). In one of the great Messianic psalms we meet a similar record, "He that dwelleth in the secret place of the most High shall abide under the shadow of the Almighty. . . . He shall cover thee with His feathers and under His wings shalt thou trust" (Ps. 91:1,4). What a wealth of weighty assurance these references minister to heart and mind! The Lord Jesus was willing to do all this for Jerusalem, but the city rejected Him. How vividly the Saviour's gracious words of invitation are recalled, "Come unto Me, all ye . . . and I will give you rest" (Matt 11:28). Every requirement of refuge, rest, renewal, and reassurance is implied in this appeal for those who respond by repairing to His presence and nestling in the nearness of His sacred bosom, a bosom that was accessible to the twelve yet only one disciple rested his head there.

> There is a place of quiet rest
>   Near to the heart of God
> A place where sin cannot molest
>   Near to the heart of God.

Of Christ it is written, "I am like a pelican of the wilderness" (Ps. 102:6). The pelican is able to penetrate more deeply into waste areas of desert lands than any other bird because it carries a substantial amount of food in the large pouch beneath the lower beak. While crossing by car the extensive desert in Iraq, we were two hundred miles southeast of Mosul when we noticed, some distance ahead, three large pelicans. We drove near enough to take a picture and while we were stopped one of the birds turned its head sideways, opened its long bill, and dropped a large pineapple on the ground. Immediately all three began pecking at the fruit and when it was considered each had had sufficient, the remainder of the pineapple was scooped into the pouch again and held in reserve. This bird is able to live for a time in the midst of surroundings that do not contribute to its maintenance.

In like manner the Son of man was not sustained from His surroundings. When in the wilderness He was challenged by the enemy and commanded to exert His creative right and secure supplies, He replied, "Man shall not live by bread alone, but by every word that proceedeth out of the mouth of God." On another occasion He said, to the surprise of His disciples, "I have meat to eat that ye know not of."

The psalm from whence our heading is taken was considered by the Church from the earliest centuries to be a description of the experiences Christ encountered in Gethsemane, and that for good reasons. On the final night which preceded the crucifixion, when He repaired to the garden He left eight of His disciples near the entrance. Three others accompanied Him some distance farther, to whom He said, "Abide ye here while I go and pray yonder." Luke records that He withdrew from them about a stone's cast. He went deeper into the depths of sorrow and suffered anguish more severely than anyone had ever done. Yea, He encountered agony more crucial, bore the heaviest of burdens, and drank the cup of woe to its direst dregs. He prevailed in this awful conflict alone, without any aid or assistance from His associates.

The singular separation and seclusion of the owl, and its nocturnal habits, naturally separate it from other winged species so that its life is lived largely in seclusion. How vividly this feature of the Saviour is expressed in the four great sorrow psalms of the Psalter. A quotation from each of the four will suffice as a demonstration. "Lover and friend hast Thou put far from me, and mine acquaintance into darkness" (Ps. 88:18). "Thou hast known my reproach and my shame, and my dishonour. . . . Reproach hath broken my heart; and I am full of heaviness: and I looked for some to take pity, but there was none; and for comforters, but I found none" (Ps. 69:19-20). "Hide not Thy face from me in the day when I am in trouble; incline Thine ear unto me: in the day when I call answer me speedily. . . . I am like an owl of the desert" (Ps. 102:2,6).

Desertion sounded the lowest depth of the Saviour's direst grief, "My God, My God, why hast Thou forsaken Me?" (Ps. 22:1) Notice the three pivots on which the first three sections of the psalm hinge, "far from Me . . . far from Me . . . far from Me" (verses 1,11,19).

The owl does not appear to be a becoming figure to use in association with so dignified a person as the Son of God, yet in this specific regard, it is the best suited of all birds to portray

Him as the One who is despised and deserted. No other member of the winged family could do so more becomingly and befittingly.

We should notice that the four birds we have mentioned thus far are chosen to set forth features that symbolized characteristics in the Son of man and experiences in His service. The three which follow signify most aptly various aspects of His sacrifice.

The dove with its mournful note suggests His sorrow as a mourner in a world of sin for which He died. The spiritual nature of Christ's sensitive soul recoiled in the presence of envy, malice, enmity, and hate, and from all other ugly propensities of which fivescore are mentioned in the New Testament. The sweetness of His spirit was never embittered by the sinister and sordid contradictions of sinners against Himself. Undoubtedly this is suggested in the figure, for the dove has no gall bladder and where there is no gall there is no bitterness.

The steadfast constancy of the Son of man is also indicated in that the divorceless dove chooses a mate and never forsakes her. The Lord has said, "I will never leave thee nor forsake thee." Furthermore, the dove builds a nest and never deserts it. Christ said explicitly, when speaking of the Father's house, "I go to prepare a place for you. . . . I will come again, and receive you unto Myself; that where I am, there ye may be also." We might rehearse the ten instructive features of the dove and find each one furnishes some special phase of the Saviour's sufficiency in the carrying out of the great plan of salvation. Let us make mention of one more of these reflections in passing. The dove's eye never winks or blinks and never shuts, for the simple reason it has no eyelid, which suggests that the eyes of our Emancipator are ever watchful in ceaseless care, for He never slumbers nor sleeps (2 Chron. 6:20; Ps. 121:4-5).

> There is an eye that never sleeps beneath the
> wing of night,
> There is an ear that never shuts when sink the
> beams of light.

We may say with assurance that in view of its nature and varied characteristics, the dove is virtuously qualified to prefigure the spiritual character that is most suitable for acceptable sacrifice and is therefore a picture of the One who is holy, guileless, and undefiled. So from the burnt offering aspect of Christ's sacrifice for adjustment down to the trespass offering for amendment under the old economy, this bird is one of the familiar figures used (Lev. 5:7,14). As Creator He has made the many creatures of His creation to supply us with graphic pictures of those secret mysteries of His grace.

Sacrificial service characterizes the pigeon. No other bird has rendered such valuable service as a messenger, or received such a variety of decorative honors for carrying dispatches as the pigeon. Thousands of them have been trained and used for army purposes. Under favorable weather conditions their flying speed is approximately sixty miles an hour.

But Christ, the swift messenger who speedily brings relief as a mediator (Luke 18), far more readily responds to a request for help and far more rapidly releases the prisoner from his bonds. Another feature of vital interest is the remarkable intelligence of the pigeon with its navigating organs which are sensitive to the earth's magnetism and rotation, and the ability it has to correlate these with its own land speed. Therefore it is able to find a way back to its loft from whence it may have been taken, even though the distance intervening be hundreds of miles. Our Saviour repeatedly emphasized that He knew full well from whence He had come and was wholly familiar with the way back and would most surely return thence. Love finds a way when none exists and He Himself founds and furnishes a way of life that leads to celestial realms. He knows the Father and is able to guide us to Him (John 14:6).

As one of the clean birds, the place the pigeon occupied in the sacrificial system of Israel is significant. Considerable impor-tance clusters round the merits of its appointment as an oblation for sin. This fact directs our thinking to the vastly superior merit of Christ's spotless character and comeliness, which adequately answers the divine claims for all human defects and deficiencies. Yes, more, His sacrifice of Himself assures an inexhaustible volume of credit which makes the bankrupt debtor solvent forevermore. The blessed, beloved and Only-begotten Son with His infinite merit has secured by His supreme sacrifice an eternal redemption.

Substitution is the key word for the sparrow. The sparrow is about the most common of birds in most lands and where a blood sacrifice was necessary for the cleansing of the leper, two were ordered to be taken by the priest for the purpose. One of these was killed and its blood taken in an earthen vessel. Then a piece of cedar, scarlet, and hyssop together with the live sparrow were dipped in the blood, and the bird was then freed and flew away with the mark of death upon it. He who said in the language of the psalm, "I am as a sparrow alone upon the housetop," is represented in this ceremony. The cedar expressed His lofty majesty, the scarlet His lovely dignity, and the hyssop His lowly humility, all figures of the true, the divine nature that constituted the sacrifice. By the symbolism of the ritual the celestial credentials of the Son of man were linked with the common sparrow. His crucifixion, resurrection, and ascension were figured in the ceremony of the cleansing of the leper. What a significance there is in the consoling word He spoke to His disciples when they were threatened with mob violence, "But even the very hairs of your head are all numbered" (Luke 12:7). He preceded this statement by saying, "Are not five sparrows sold for two farthings?" (verse 6) The cheapest of the sacrifices, to all outward seeming, had behind it the costliest and choicest celestial values, because as the Redeemer He was therein represented as the lone sparrow. By virtue of the infinite price He paid as a ransom for them every hair was of value to Him.

Such pictures portray a profound expression of Emmanuel's qualifications in discharging His many-sided ministry, the range of which extends from His exalted status of being loftiest in sovereignty as signified in the eagle, to the place of lowliest submission as suggested in the sparrow. His adaptability to the conditions for ratifying the covenant and His suitability in answering every legal demand and fulfilling every righteous obligation are beyond question.

The lists of representative birds and representative beasts in Scripture are brought before our notice to verify an important truth in relation to substitutionary sacrifice. Christ was not slain in this province as a private individual, but was put to death as a representative man: "Because we thus judge that if one died for all, then all died" (2 Cor. 5:14 ASR). On the occasion when Christ offered Himself without spot, He was accepted in the character of that capacity in which God regarded Him from before the foundation of the world. By His manifestation He assumed the position of being the second Man and therefore the last Adam, and did what He did as the covenant Head and federal Representative of mankind. Therefore, however gross and grievous the insults may be that a merciful and faithful God has suffered because of the enormity of sin's guilt, the sacrifice which Christ made and the price He paid with the infinite merit of His perfect character brought inconceivably majestic recompense and immortal honor to eternal justice. The glories of His peerless personality furnish values inestimable and merit incalculable, which far outweigh the discredit done to God's radiant name and the dishonor brought upon His regnant love.

Even to *suggest* a boundary or to *suppose* a limit to the incomparable efficacy of His unrivaled sacrifice is an insult to infinite wisdom.

THE ORACLE OF GOD

God, who at sundry times and in divers manners spake in times past unto the fathers by the prophets, Hath in these last days spoken unto us by His Son, whom He hath appointed heir of all things (Heb. 1:1-2).

I speak to the world those things which I have heard of Him (John 8:26).

I speak that which I have seen with My Father (John 8:38).

For I have not spoken of Myself; but the Father which sent Me,

He gave me a commandment, what I should say, and what I should speak. . . . Whatsoever I speak therefore, even as the Father said unto Me, so I speak (John 12:49-50).

The words that I speak to you I speak not from Myself (John 14:10).

Sixteen references are made in the Old Testament writings to the oracle of the Temple, and half of these occur in 1 Kings 6, where a detailed account is given of its exquisite beauty and golden glory.

The distinctive structure was designed as a speaking chamber and was also known as the holy of holies wherein the divine glory resided. The interior measured twenty by twenty by twenty cubits, the length, breadth, and height being equal. Two large cherubim of ten cubits were carved from olive wood, each with two wings five cubits in length, and covered with beaten gold. These were placed in the golden chamber. Between the two cherubim that had their wings outspread the ark of the covenant was set, and its mercy seat of pure gold was directly under the spot where the tips of the two inner wings of the cherubim met. From the first reference to these beings in the Bible, we learn that they represented divine justice (Gen 2:24), while their covering of beaten gold symbolized divine righteousness, and the combination of these attributes which are so plainly expressed in Scripture, is confidently asserted by the Apostle Paul when he speaks of the righteous judgment of God. The entire oracle both as to its character and contents was divinely designed to represent the inherent nature of the indescribable Christ.

The whole interior of this sacred chamber was overlaid with pure gold, including the floor, ceiling, and walls. The stonework within was first covered with cedar and cypress woods on which were carvings of cherubim, palms, and open flowers. This ornamental woodwork was then overlaid with beaten gold so that not a trace of the natural features of the wood and stone was left visible. The carved figures on the walls reflected the matchless perfections, moral beauties, manifold graces, and magnificent glories of Christ's inner nature that were obscured from out-ward observation. Moreover, the majestic sovereignty of His kingly dignity was expressed in the crown of gold on the ark, His merciful sympathy was foreshadowed in the precious mercy seat, while His multiform sufficiency was signified in the con-tents of the ark.

Let us recall that Aaron's rod that budded was there, which in figure, added the triumph of resurrection power to His sover-eignty. Also the tables of the Law were within, a law which Christ magnified and made honorable, which suggests that His life of replete perfection supports His sympathetic pity. We are well aware that compassion if based upon corruption cannot continue, whereas His compassion being founded on perfection continues ever. The third feature of the ark's content was the pot of manna, a perpetual reminder that resourceful provision for His redeemed hosts is included in His sufficiency. We re-member His declaration, "I am that bread of life. . . . If any man eat of this bread, he shall live forever" (John 6:48,50).

The graphic description that is given relative to the scintillat-ing beauties of the brilliant, radiant, flashing, effulgent beams of lustrous golden light in luminous transcendence within the oracle, is but a faint foreshadowing of the ineffable glory real-ized and reflected in the everlasting Word, which was made flesh and dwelt among us. John declares, "[and we beheld His glory, the glory as of the only begotten of the Father,] full of grace and truth" (John 1:14). A sight of the Son who was sent by the Father, this pictorial vision of the inward purity and perfection of His virtuous character should thrill and fill the soul with admiring wonder and adoring worship.

Let us be mindful of the fact, that when the Lord spoke to the nation of Israel, He did so from between the cherubim, whose outspread wings reached from wall to wall of the oracle, so that the inner wings met in the midst of the chamber. Right beneath, where the wings touched one another, was the mercy seat on which the blood of atonement was sprinkled. Atonement means to cover up or cover over sin. This was achieved by the blood of beasts, but the blood of Christ has accomplished much more than this. He entered not into the holy places made with hands, but into Heaven itself (Heb. 9:24). His sacrifice of Himself has secured eternal redemption with its everlasting reconciliation. Sin has been expunged and eliminated and all evidence of guilt erased, so that by Him we are justified from all things. Therefore His blood speaks, yea, speaketh better things.

Because of the conquest gained at Calvary, His cross has been made the central tribunal for the administration of judgment, and the Father has committed all judgment to the Son (John 5:22). When Christ was interpreting the cause and reason for the delegation of supreme justice to His hands, after signifying by what manner of death He would glorify God, He added, "Now is the judgment of this world: now shall the prince of this world be cast out. And I, if I be lifted up . . . will draw all unto Me" (John 12:31-32). "Men" is not in the text. Our Lord is not speaking here of drawing for salvation, but for justice. Everyone of all men and all movements will be drawn to one central tribunal for judgment, where the Oracle of God will speak the final verdict.

Under the Old Testament symbolism a conclusive confirmation is given of this judicial function. The area of the brazen altar is exactly the same as that of the oracle, twenty by twenty cubits, but it was half the height which caused the sacrifice offered thereon to be centered. The offering on the brazen altar stands for righteousness, while the cherubim of the oracle bespeak judgment. Christ is both Offering and Oracle, both the righteousness of God and the judgment of God are coordinated in His complete character.

The blood of the offering that was brought by the high priest of Israel and sprinkled on the golden mercy seat beneath the wings of the cherubim was a preview of the cross and predictive of the mighty transaction that would there take place.

The graphic portrayal sets forth pictorially that at Golgotha divine justice would stand with her gleaming sword triumphant, but divine mercy would sway her golden scepter, regnant in sublimest splendor. The oracle therefore issues a new commanding order that repentance and remission of sins be preached to all nations in His Name.

> In the Cross of Christ I glory, towering o'er the wrecks of time,
> All the light of sacred story gathers round its head sublime.

Elizabeth Clephane of Fireshire, Scotland, stated this supreme matter in her profound hymn which begins with the words, "Beneath the Cross of Jesus." The second verse reads:

> O safe and happy shelter! O refuge tried and sweet!
> O trysting place, where heaven's *love*
> and heaven's *justice* meet.
> As to the pilgrim patriarch that wondrous dream was given,
> So seems my Saviour's cross to me, a ladder up to Heaven.

Or, as stated in the words of Samuel Rutherford of Ainsworth:

> With *mercy* and with *judgment* my
> web of time He wove
> And aye the dews of sorrow were lustered
> with His love
> I'll bless the hand that guided,
> I'll bless the heart that planned
> When throned where glory dwelleth
> in Immanuel's land.

In the light of this omniscient One offering Himself through the eternal Spirit without spot, in order to silence the demands of justice and satisfy the claims of righteousness against sin, must not the voice of the Vindicator be the most charming and consoling ever heard? How wonderful it must be to hear Him speak to the world as the Oracle of God, for God has spoken in His Son. Should we not hang on His words as we listen to His saying, "As Moses lifted up the serpent in the wilderness, even so must the Son of man be lifted up: That whosoever believeth in Him should not perish, but have eternal life. For God so loved the world, that He gave His only begotten Son, that whosoever believeth in Him should not perish, but have everlasting life" (John 3:14-16)? And again, "If any man thirst let him come unto Me and drink." Never man spoke like this man for He is God's divine Oracle, whose words have never been equaled, let alone excelled. We might well spend hours on this theme of endless profit.

Let us rehearse one other statement that He made at the close of His wonderful prayer: "O righteous Father, the world hath not known Thee: but I have known Thee, and these have known that Thou hast sent Me. And I have declared unto them Thy name, and will declare it: that the love wherewith Thou hast loved Me may be in them, and I in them" (John 17:25-26). No one, either before or since, has used such language as this. The words "righteous" and "Father" verify what has been mentioned under the present heading.

Righteous implies one that is unswerving, undeviating, and unrelenting in justice, but Father includes unlimited, unbounded, unrestricted mercy along with it. Christ came to manifest the Father whose holy law demands that His perfect justice be vindicated and with this demand justly met, decrees and declares by virtue of His heavenly love that the offer of perfect justification to the offenders be vouchsafed. On the sole basis of Christ's sacrifice of Himself this has been realized, and the Mediator becomes the mouthpiece of God to record and report the finished work, and to speak forth God's final word on forgiveness.

Forasmuch then as the Son in His glorious character of godhead knows the Father in a distinctive, exclusive, and superlative sense, He came to declare Him in all His glorious greatness and generous grace. As being perfectly qualified with His immortal knowledge and insight our Saviour was manifested to impart instruction to mankind and make clear the magnificence of the immemorial Name, to the intent that we might understand somewhat of the Father's immutable love for Him and His for us. As God's Oracle He said, "As the Father hath loved Me, so have I loved you" (John 15:9).

New values of inestimable fame are added to love's gracious might and glorious measure by virtue of His amazing friendship and fellowship with humanity. No subject is more suitable, serviceable, and seasonable at all times than love. The correlatives "as" and "so" that are used here by the Lord are weighted with golden wealth, heavenly treasure, and celestial riches, as reflected in the sublime structures of the oracle. We fail to grasp the immortal tenderness of these words as we, in faith, would comprehend their immaculate truthfulness. The ten thousand times ten thousand love deeds of His life and the transporting transcendence of His triumphal death express the tideless fullness of His faithful constancy which confirms conclusively His pregnant words, "So have I loved you." This assurance reaches the supremest degree of sublime dimension.

The Name He reveals includes in its range all the features and characteristics of will, work, word, and wisdom by which a person may be described. Christ has discharged all this as God's Oracle and has declared, in measure, the fathomless marvels of the Father's ever-enduring Name, the nature of which is altogether incorruptible and immutable. All judgment and all justification have been committed to the Son, who now exhibits all the prerogatives of a faithful judge and exercises every potential and principle of a flawless justice. Possessed of every essential attribute of deity, there can be no defect in His discernment of right and wrong, truth and error, or good and evil. In revealing of the name of the invisible godhead, in resembling the nature of the incorruptible God and in representing the nobility of the infinite majesty of the heavens in His oral message, He is without compare.

In lieu of what He achieved by His sacrifice and in view of the blessings He administers by virtue of His sovereignty, He is equally just when pardoning a repentant soul as when punishing a rebellious sinner. Many of this world's thinkers endeavor to play upon the sympathetic susceptibilities of the people to stir up their pity for those punished, but few there are who teach men to abhor the obnoxious evil that inevitably draws forth the deserved penalty. This world's philosophy looks upon the record of God's Oracle in figure and fact with contempt, but the saved recognize that the substance of the elaborate symbolism is Christ, the Power of God, the Wisdom of God, the Justice of God, and the Oracle of God.

God hath spoken unto us by His Son, who yet speaketh. He speaketh still, list to His words. He showeth still, look for His lessons. He serveth still, ask for His aid. Ponder His precepts, study His statutes. Consider His commands, place the highest value on the voice of His Word. He it is who speaks as the beloved Son to His brethren, as the Bridegroom to His bride, and as the blessed and only Potentate to the blessed of the Father. Yea, He still speaks on God's behalf as the Shepherd to the sheep, as the Saviour to the saints, and as the Sovereign to the subjects of the everlasting kingdom.

THE OMEGA

I am Alpha and Omega (Rev. 22:13).

Christ in His Lordship does something unprecedented in history when He adopts the final letter of the famous Greek alphabet as a title. In His wisdom He combines with it the first letter, *alpha,* which makes both His name and claim stupendous and supernatural. So we learn from this that Christ is not only final in the entire world of wisdom and knowledge, but He is also foremost. Immediately after making this amazing statement to John He added the additional announcement, "I am the root and offspring of David, the bright, the morning star." He precedes and succeeds David, likewise He is not merely the sign of each new dawn as the Morning Star, but is the significant mark of every approaching night of darkness as the Evening Star, for these are not two different stars, but one and the same. So also the title First and Last refers to one and the same Person. The

Beginning and the End denotes one and the same Christ. The Alpha and Omega declares one and the same Revealer. The Author and Perfector specifies one and the same Lord.

Where may we look for another character such as this, who, as the Ancient of Days, is anterior to all time, and as the Almighty, is posterior to all that is temporal, because of His timeless authority. Let us bear in mind we are considering a living, loving being who is the innermost center of divine purity, the outermost circle of divine plenty, the uppermost crown of divine pity, and the uttermost claim of divine parity. The sum total of desirability and durability and the subsistence of dignity and deity reside in Him, yea, all the fullness of godhead bodily (Col. 2:9).

We are all familiar with the expression, "Oh, yes, Dr. So and So is the last word in medical science or mathematical skill," or we hear it said that a specific watch is the last word in accuracy and elegancy as a timepiece. In the present case Christ is the last letter in the alphabet of the language of revealed truth, of spiritual knowledge, and of divine wisdom. He is not only president in all that is first and chief, but preeminent in all that is final and complete.

He outlives, outlasts, and outloves all the lofty and lustrous of history. Christ in His exclusive personality characterizes the radiance of the light of truth, He comprises the reservoir of the life of truth. He constitutes the residence of the love of truth and He compasses the rendezvous of the law of truth. The primal supremacy and potential superiority are not formal but final propensities, not temporal but eternal prerogatives.

This unique name Omega is suitably appropriated by One who is the chiefest in leadership and lordship, the choicest in headship and heirship, and the comeliest in superlative kingship and superior judgeship. Is it possible to suggest a more unusual title for the Chief of celebrities and Prince of potentates? Christ Himself coined and claimed the name as a personal designation, and within the significant confines of His undefinable merits, the use which He makes of it suggests among other wonders that He is the Bond and Boundary of all immutability in both creation and covenants.

He is the Center and Circumference of all immortality in both desirability and durability. He is the Sum and Summit of all immensity in both greatness and goodness. Yea, He is the Zone and Zenith of all immeasurability of both perfection and preeminence. The very position held by the vowel *omega* at the close of the Greek alphabet is indicative of the important influence Christ exercises as the sole executor of the divine will, which is one of the main features of Revelation. He it is who concludes the essential plan of giving gifts, Himself the most priceless gift ever bestowed. He also completes the entire program of grace so that "of His fulness have all we received, and grace for grace" (John 1:16). He it is who confirms the whole casket of promise, "all the promises of God in Him are yea" (2 Cor. 1:20). He consummates the eternal purpose of God, for in Him all things are to be gathered together in one (Eph. 1:10).

The suggestiveness of the symbolism Christ here calls into requisition by the use of this last letter is remarkable, as reflecting His supreme supervisory station of control over all that has gone before. "Thou remainest," is twice stated in Scripture of the One who abides when all else recedes. "Thou, O Lord, remainest for ever" (Lam. 5:19; Heb. 1:11). Amid an environment of perpetual change, "Thou art the same," (Heb. 1:12). In an atmosphere of continual variation Thou art without variableness or shadow of turning (Jas. 1:17). Encompassed by the transient surroundings of temporal things with their fluctuation and fatigue, "Thou faintest not and art never weary, Thou upholdest all things by the word of Thy power."

Omega is therefore a title of the Lord's own coinage, minted so as to reflect His image, engraved so as to declare His rights, inscribed so as to reveal His character, designed so as to denote His claims, molded so as to magnify His name, and placed in the vocabulary of Scripture for circulation, in order to remind mankind of His age-abiding sovereignty. This prominent designation signifies the deathless realities of His wisdom, the ceaseless resources of His knowledge, and the ageless superiority He holds over all others and all else. In this capacity He is the entity of essential excellence and the eternity of celestial effulgence. What a magnificent portrayal of personality is hereby expressed when we visualize our Lord standing at the terminus of time with adequate power to turn the stream of human history and national authority into the channel of a new destiny for the establishment in manifestation of His everlasting kingdom.

As the Omega, Christ is the terminal fullness of revealed truth, the Climax of complete comprehension, the Summit of absolute sufficiency in understanding, the Promoter of perfect knowledge, and the wonderful Counselor of replete wisdom. In this supernatural status He administers without the remotest trace of a rival, without the faintest sign of an equal, and without the slightest possibility of anyone ever arising to excel, because He is final in being and personality as the Last, the End, the Omega.

The imagery He uses in these figures of speech betokens a resourcefulness that is boundless, exhaustless, reckonless, and becomes increasingly wonderful the more it is contemplated. The relevancy of the title which He so rightfully assumes serves as an index and an appendix to the infinities of His matchless Being.

A Christ so wondrous and worshipful is in Himself the Finality of God's truth, the Immensity of God's might, the Constancy of God's love, the Infinity of God's grace, the Stability of God's peace, the Tranquility of God's rest, and the Sublimity of God's glory.

The mountains of vision which dominate the landscape of Palestine also furnish a definite contribution in depicting the magnificent majesty of Messiah the Prince. They constitute visible emblems of His greater invisible grandeur, and serve as material witnesses in directing our thoughts to the moral heights of spiritual splendor on the horizons of glory. Ten of these are familiar to all those who read the Scriptures.

Memorable Mount Moriah, from whence the patriarchal prediction was made that God would provide Himself a lamb for a burnt offering, supplies the famous forecast which was so graphically fulfilled by Christ, who, as the I AM, receded Abraham (John 8:58). From the meaning of the title which originated from Jehovah Jireh, we derive the assured forecast, "In the mount of the Lord it shall be seen."

From the heights of magnificent Horeb the Lord revealed to Moses the plan and purpose of salvation, which salvation was eventually expressed in the Person of the Son of God, who unveiled a vaster vision (Luke 2:30; 19:9).

From majestic Sinai, amid gorgeous splendor, the moral law was revealed, that same which Messiah fulfilled, magnified and made honorable, redeeming mankind from its curse and condemnation, in order to ratify a New Covenant.

Mournful Mount Hor was the burial place of Aaron, Israel's first official high priest, which supplies a constant reminder that our great High Priest Jesus liveth and abideth forever, and continually maketh intercession for us, whereby He is able to save to the uttermost (Heb. 7:25), by virtue of His indestructible priesthood.

Matchless Pisgah is the mount from whose summit Moses saw the land of promise, and which in figure we ascend to view the land of the far distances, even the inheritance incorruptible, with its breadth and length and depth and height (Eph. 3:18).

Monumental Tabor is the sentinel of the historic plain of Esdraelon and the notable watchtower of Deborah; the mount is believed by some to have been the scene of the transfiguration, and if so, is the standpoint from whence a glimpse of the coming kingdom was granted to three of the disciples (2 Pet. 1:18).

Maritime Carmel, on the shore of the Mediterranean Sea, is the precise locality where the forces of idolatry were frustrated and subdued, a signal sign of the subjugating power of a risen Christ, triumphing over the obdurate foe.

The bastions of mighty Zion formed the marshal citadel of David's significant reign, which presages the kingly sovereignty of David's greater Son, swaying the scepter over nations, peoples, and tongues forevermore.

Massive Hermon, first mentioned by Moses, is the great monitor of the north, within the shadow of whose lofty peak Christ stood when He asked His challenging question in Caesarea Philippi, "Whom do ye say that I am?" and received the heaven-revealed reply from Peter's lips, "Thou art the Christ, the Son of the living God." What a matchless setting for so memorable an event!

Finally, there is momentous Olivet, the scene of the ascension, depicting our blessed Lord in His kingly beauty and kindly blessing beyond the reach of death, the grand token of ultimate triumph over the crushing grief and cruelty of the grave.

Each of these historical mountains makes a manifold contribution to the memories of revealed truth, but towering highest, shining brightest, sounding loudest, and echoing clearest are the light waves and bright rays of divine wisdom and knowledge broadcast from the names and titles of our blessed Saviour whose creative power they portray. Every one of these designations is an everlasting monument of heavenly mercy and holy majesty.

The Scriptures plainly reveal the perfect manner in which our Lord fills every high office and fulfills every obligation committed to Him. The Word of God unfolds a masterful variety of vocations with far-reaching issues, all of which He thoroughly and triumphantly discharges. His names are like a garden of perennial flowers, His ministries like a perpetual stream of fragrance and His permanent majesty and prevailing magnificence never vary in righteousness or resoluteness.

He ever reigns amid the unwaning glory of God in an unending kingdom, draped in translucent splendor and drenched in greater grandeur than all former rulers, for He is high above all other principalities and powers, whatever their might and dominion (Eph. 1:21). Our noblest comprehension of Christ is extremely paltry, and is far less in proportion than a cupful of water in comparison with the ocean, tinier than a spark in relation to a full-orbed sun, yea, smaller in degree than an inch might be beside the trackless leagues of infinite space.

When we take into account the extensive range of our Lord's princely offices, and consider the expansive reign of His perfect omnipotence, and combine these with the exclusive renown of His personal omniscience, we may well ask:

What is the eternal kingdom without the essential King?
What is the scepter of might without the superior Majesty?
What is the nation's homeland without the notable Heir?
What is the holy city without the heavenly Christ?
What is the bridal beauty without the beloved Bridegroom?
What is the pledged estate without the prince Emmanuel?
What is the sacred sanctuary without the sanctifying Saviour?
What is the temple ritual without the revealed Truth?
What is the promised covenant without the personal Christ?
What is the living hope without the Lover Himself?
What is the passing shadow without the permanent Substance?
What is the gift of mercy without the gracious Mediator?
What is the eternal redemption without the eternal Redeemer?
What is the prophetic message without the predicted Messiah?

If these questions are thought to be trifling, may we ask another one, can the Lord of life ever be deposed or the Lord of lords dethroned or the Lord of love displaced?

We should forever remind ourselves that invincible might and inconceivable majesty form the background of Christ's inestimable mercy and inimitable ministry. We should recognize that irrefutable revelation and impregnable righteousness are the bastions of His irrevocable purpose and irresistible power. We should remember that infinite constancy and inherent superiority stand behind His immortal sympathy and incorruptible sufficiency. We should recall that ineffable glory and immaculate goodness secure the bounty of His inexhaustible grace and insuperable gifts.

What a concentration of distinctive capacities and what a centralization of exclusive capabilities are found in Christ Jesus our Lord! Not one of these qualities is fragmentary, each is final and full-orbed. Such a galaxy of glories was never before seen in so suitable and notable a setting. Is there anything worthwhile in wisdom or wealth that Christ does not have? Is there any phase of honorable experience or noble endurance He did not enter? Is there any spiritual excellence or effluence He did not express?

Under what circumstances was Christ ever cramped by disability when He turned attention to act in connection with the material, physical, and ethical realms? Under what environment was He curtailed by debility when exercising His will in the social, racial, or national spheres? Under what conditions was He circumscribed by deficiency when administering in the moral, spiritual, or judicial arenas? Moreover, Christ is the only Mediator existing who wields the power to unify the factions of diverse systems that lead to disunion in this war-riven world, and is the sole Arbiter in the universe who can harmonize all forms of disparity that lead to disaffection and disruption. Nor has He left us in doubt as to the ultimate and final issues. "Having made known unto us the mystery of His will, according to His good pleasure which He hath purposed in Himself: that in the dispensation of the fulness of times He might gather together in one all things in Christ, both which are in heaven, and which are on earth; even in Him" (Eph. 1:9-10). What unanimity is this! What a union! What a unification! What a unity!